The Grief Book

Strategies for Young People

Elizabeth Vercoe
Kerry Abramowski

16

EasyRead Large

Copyright Page from the Original Book

First published in 2004 by

black dog books

15 Gertrude Street
Fitzroy Vic 3065
Australia
61 + 3 + 9419 9406
61 + 3 + 9419 1214 (fax)
dog@bdb.com.au

Designed by Blue Boat Design
Cover photograph: Getty Images
Printed and bound in Australia by Griffin Press

Vercoe, Elizabeth, 1967- .
The grief book : strategies for young people.

For children 12 years and over.
ISBN 1 876372 52 4.

1. Grief - Juvenile literature. 2. Grief in children - Juvenile literature. 3. Bereavement in children - Juvenile literature. I. Abramowski, Kerry. II. Title.

155.937

For the person who smiles at a stranger as they walk along the street.
For the person with an outstretched hand.
For the person who takes that hand.
For my incredible family and friends.
Elizabeth Vercoe

To Cyndi, Dillon, Diz, Gab, Prof, Simon and Ogleberry for your support, friendship and wisdom. My own bag of tricks grows heavier and stronger because of you all.
Kerry Abramowski

TABLE OF CONTENTS

A bag of tricks – coping strategies

Feeling grief and loss is very necessary. It happens to us all. Someone in your family might be ill. You might be ill yourself. Your parents might be separated or divorced. You might be looking for your birth parents. You might feel like you're not good enough, or have really hard things to deal with.

It's okay to be sad sometimes. It happens to us all. It's what we do with our sadness that matters.

This is a book full of ideas, anecdotes, stories, quotes and hands-on exercises. Tricks to survive. Coping strategies to use in everyday life when you're feeling sad, or angry, or guilty, or helpless, or maybe just nothing.

There are many different tricks. Some can be used just as they are. Others you can weave together according to your needs. All the tricks are user-friendly. Some of these tricks you'll hold close to your heart because they will work for you. Others might not be for you.

At its heart, this book is really 'a bag of tricks'. It is best read from cover to cover, but may be dipped into as required. Take the tricks in this book and put them in an (imaginary) bag, sling it over your shoulder and carry it throughout your life. Use the tricks when you need them. They'll always be there.

Our intent is to offer you hope, strength, inspiration, courage, and maybe even a smile or two, in your time of need.

Elizabeth Vercoe (author) and Kerry Abramowski (consultant)

What is grief?

Grief is a sign that we loved something more than ourselves.

Joan Chittister

Here is a dictionary version:

Grief: n: 1. Keen mental suffering or distress over affliction or loss; sharp sorrow; painful regret.

For me, grief is lots of different things.

It is that sinking feeling in the pit of your stomach that you go to sleep with and wake up with.

It is the tears rolling down your face as you wash the dishes, walk down the street or sip a cappuccino.

It is not being able to say what you want to say.

It is wishing that you were somewhere else; never being comfortable anywhere.

It is clutching and grasping at memories.

It is violent mood swings – kicking the kitchen cupboard with all your strength and then weeping uncontrollably curled up on the floor.

It is screaming and wailing into your cornflakes.

It is long walks to nowhere in particular.

It is endless cups of tea and visitors.

It is going to the driving range and belting 200 golf balls.

It is scatteredness, the inability to concentrate and the need to do something all the time – or vice versa.

It is not remembering who you've seen lately.

It is hysterical laughter at inappropriate times.

It is obsession with cleanliness or cake baking.

It is overwhelming.

It is all-consuming.

It is guilt when you forget about it for even a moment.

It is a tidal wave breaking over you.

It is never-ending.

It is everything.

It is impossible.

Ultimately, each of us experiences grief in our own personal way. We are all unique. No two people can live exactly the same life. The tapestry that we each weave is as unique as our fingerprints and our smiles. The grief I describe may not be your grief. There's one thing I know for certain – grief is a doorway to be stepped through.

My story – elizabeth vercoe

Sometimes grief can be so black it is difficult to see out of it to a time when you will feel better. It's helpful to know that others have grieved before you and made it through. This is my story.

A profound journey began for me in 1992 when I was diagnosed with Hodgkin's Disease – a cancer of the lymphatic system. I spent a lot of time and energy pretending I wasn't sick, and I felt angry and guilty inside. All my reactions were aspects of grief, but I didn't know this at the time. I was trying very hard to stay normal and to pretend that nothing was happening, even though I was having radiation treatment, taking strong pain killers and feeling awful. I began to work harder and longer hours as an actor and musician. All my life I had dreamed of doing this work and I wasn't going to let a little thing like cancer stop me! Or so I thought.

But, you can't run away from yourself. Not for long anyway. And the cancer returned to my body. Partly, I think this happened because I was refusing to look at the feelings and emotions that were trapped within me.

When finally I acknowledged my fear, it was one year later. I was lying in traction in a hospital bed gravely ill, and finally my grieving process was able to begin.

I grieved through surgery which saved my life. Doctors took bones from my leg and hip, and used metal rods and bits of wire to replace much of my upper spine that had been eaten away.

I grieved through chemotherapy, hair loss, the loss of my voice, loss of my normal bodily functions such as feeding myself and going to the toilet, loss of independence, loss of the use of my legs and arm.

I grieved for my happy little house, and for my family and friends.

I grieved for the future I had dreamed of.

I grieved for my life as I had known it. Not as a general thing, but for all of the parts, individually, which made up my life.

And over the months, as I wept and became less physically dependent – less like a helpless baby – I began to heal. Somewhere during that eternal time, I looked deeply into the darkness inside (even though I didn't want to) and acknowledged that I was afraid.

Afraid of dying, and now, afraid of living. What if I never got out of hospital?

I was also grieving for all that I had lost. I was grieving over old wounds, like my parents' marriage breakdown years earlier. I was grieving for a friend who had died in grade two. For failed relationships. For my inadequacies. And for every disappointment or feeling of 'not being good enough' that I had ever felt.

In short, I had opened up a place within me that had been closed down for a long time. It was a slow and painful process. At times it felt like torture.

I wept. Hours every day for months on end. And even now, I weep. I am moved often. Sometimes I cry as I watch my three young children smear vegemite all over the wall. I cry because it's a miracle that they are here on the earth at all, as I wasn't expected to be able to have children. There was also doubt as to whether I would walk again. I can work up to a slow jog these days if I'm careful!

Grieving has been a huge and pivotal part of my healing. And now, I am able to identify that when I am having a sad feeling or being unkind, it is often connected to an aspect of grief. This aspect may be a situation or a person – it really doesn't matter. Whether big or small, I am learning to acknowledge my feelings. This opens the way for them to be released.

Tricks

Trick #1 are you grieving?

Are you grieving? It's time to find out. One of the trickiest things about grief is that it can sneak up on you. It might take time to figure out that you're grieving. Acknowledging this can be very difficult because the next step means that you have to take an honest look at what's going on inside. And it ain't always pretty in there.

Grieving checklist

Read through the following list and take an honest look at what you're doing and how you're feeling. To answer yes to a question, place a tick in the box beside it. Otherwise, leave the box blank.

Are you more tired than usual?   —

Do you get grumpy with people more often than usual?   —

Do you feel like smashing something fragile?   —

Do you feel unusually lonely?   —

Do you want to talk to someone about something but just can't _
quite manage it?

Are you eating a lot more or less than usual?   —

Do you find yourself asking 'why' a lot?   —

Are you suddenly feeling vulnerable?   —

Do you feel that you have no control over what happens to you? —

Do you feel that you just don't want to be around people, that you want to be by yourself a lot? ⎯

Do you flare up and feel like hitting out at people? ⎯

Are you using drugs and/or alcohol to numb your feelings? ⎯

Do you feel like everything is 'hopeless'? ⎯

Do you feel numb, like everything is going on around you but you're not really there? ⎯

Do you miss something or someone so much that it physically hurts? ⎯

Are you doubting yourself, or feeling like you're worthless? ⎯

Table 4.1

If you have ticked some, most or all of these questions, then you may be experiencing a grief reaction. Here are some normal grief reactions.

Emotions

Anxiety and fear
Sadness
Anger
Guilt
Inadequacy
Hurt
Relief
Loneliness

Physical sensations

Hollowness in stomach
Tightness in chest
Tightness in throat

Over-sensitivity to noise
A feeling that you're not present, life's a dream
Breathlessness, feeling short of breath
Weakness of muscles
Lack of energy
Dry mouth

Thoughts

Disbelief
Confusion
Preoccupation
Sense of presence
Hallucinations

Behaviours

Sleep disturbances
Appetite disturbances
Absent-minded behaviour
Social withdrawal
Dreams of what or who has been lost
Avoiding reminders of the loss
Searching and calling out to someone who's not there
Sighing
Restless over-activity
Crying
Visiting places and carrying objects that remind you of the loss

Treasuring objects that are associated with the loss

Grief can cause your behaviour to change. Sometimes, things you do might become more pronounced or exaggerated – you might speak louder, jiggle your foot more quickly, chew your nails, or get really pissed off at nothing at all. This is normal. People who are grieving can be very different from their normal selves.

Of course you will be affected and changed by grief – it's sort of obvious. When you deal with any crisis you can expect that there will be change. It's the same when you grieve. The changes in you can be quick and dramatic and, because of this, scary.

Grief is isolating, it can be very depressing and at times it's downright frightening. Some pretty annoying things can happen too. When you are feeling alone and vulnerable, other unhappy emotions from the past may come back to bother you. On top of coping with your present grief, you might have to deal with old feelings of guilt, or abandonment, or whatever else it is that keeps you up at night.

In grief, it's normal to feel very sad and to experience a huge sense of loss. It's also normal that different situations will bring up the same grief feelings such as anger and loss.

Grief is a deep, sometimes life-changing experience that every person will encounter at some time in their lives.

It's important to identify when you are grieving, because if you don't know what's happening you can't fix it.

Trick #2 looking after yourself

Deep peace of the running wave to you
Deep peace of the flowing air to you
Deep peace of the quiet earth to you
Deep peace of the shining stars to you
Deep peace of the gentle night to you
Moon and stars pour their healing light on you
Deep peace to you

a traditional Gaelic blessing

The following ideas may seem indulgent, but they are essential for a healthy and balanced body and mind.

There are many weird and wonderful ways that you can rest. By giving your body some time-out from the tension which often accompanies grief, you allow for healing to take place.

One of the best ways to heal when you are tired and stressed is to sleep. Unfortunately, if your body is rigid and tense then sleep is often the last place it will go. The good news is that there are loads of drug-free ways to help you settle and relax.

Why not try a few of these ideas and you may be relaxed in no time at all.

A bath. A beautiful, deep, rejuvenating bath. Pop in some essential oils which you can buy from health food or body shops. Lavender, chamomile and bergamot are good for relaxation and healing. Just a few drops are needed.

Light some candles and turn off your lights. Watch the flames. Watch the shadows flicker on the wall.

If you're not into having a bath but still feel like some aromatherapy, you can burn essential oils in a burner (get these where you buy the oil) or you can dab a little lavender on some pulse points – your wrists, neck, inner elbows and the sides of your forehead. Essential oils are pretty strong, so apart from a couple of drops of lavender, avoid direct contact with skin and keep them away from your eyes.

A good book in a comfy chair with a warm drink is always a winner in my house. The healing and relaxing properties of a good book have long been established.

A head massage. A large percentage of the body's nerve endings are found in the forehead. Place your palm on your brow and consciously relax the muscles around your eyes and in your whole face. A gentle smoothing and stroking of this area by someone you feel comfortable with, or by yourself, can release tension and promote warmth and relaxation.

The feet are a great part of the body to pamper. Have a nice foot soak – some warm water, lavender oil and marbles in the bowl to massage your feet. Or slice up a lemon and float the pieces in your foot bath.

If you're feeling brave, try a foot rub. Tickly, but worth it!

Nature is another way to soothe the body and mind.

Sunsets from a high viewing point are awe-inspiring. Sunsets from your street or doorstep aren't too shabby either. They take us into a bigger realm where it is possible to forget our problems – even if it's just for a moment.

Open fires are hypnotic. Watch the flames as they leap and curl about the logs.

The ocean or a river. To watch water moving and the light dancing as it flickers and reflects the sun can take your mind into a gentle and healing place.

If you've never seen the sky at night, go out into your backyard or, if you can, get away from the city lights, take a journey and lose yourself in the stars.

If you can't do any of those things where you live, then create your own sanctuary. It can be quite small and still work. A bedroom is ideal. Stick up posters of forests and waterways. Cover your ceiling with glow-in-the-dark stars. Build your own water feature or get one from a plant nursery. Make it cosy and safe. Play your favourite music. Be still and quiet. Write in your journal. Do some nice things for yourself.

A table, a chair, a bowl of fruit and a violin. What else does a man need to be happy?

Albert Einstein

Nurture yourself, in whatever ways you can. This won't solve grief, but it will help you to move through it. Take some time for yourself. Enjoy it. You deserve it.

Trick #3 watch out for bad tricks

Bad tricks include things like blaming, bullying, denial (time-out is okay), hurting yourself, suicide, revenge/retaliation, eating disorders, dependence on drugs and alcohol, isolating yourself (again, time-out is okay), not looking after yourself.

These may seem like a way out, but in fact they are very harmful. Bad tricks stop you coping with your grief and it's easy to become lost when you use them. They're often 'bandaid' solutions – they cover up a problem for a while but don't last. They can hurt you and hurt other people. And the other thing is that they don't work. They'll keep you stuck in your grief.

If you are using bad tricks and want some help, talk to a trusted adult (see trick #10) There are people around with lots of experience who can help.

Also, there are a few medical conditions – depression is a major one – which have similar symptoms to those associated with grief. See a doctor, counsellor or other health professional if you require further information on this.

Trick #4 grief experts

I started teaching in a secondary school when I was quite young and I really enjoyed it. In my first week as a teacher I was asked to leave the staff room a couple of times – some of the teachers thought I was a student.

I didn't know much about tricks back then and so I didn't have one to use when a really sad event happened at the school.

I'd been away for a couple of days (with the flu, I think) and when I returned to school I heard – in our morning staff meeting – that one of my students had died the previous day. It was very tragic. He had thrown himself in front of a train.

Nothing can prepare you for hearing news like that. So, slowly and mechanically, I picked up my attendance book and began the short walk to class assembly.

My class were quiet that morning. Strangely, they were waiting outside the room instead of lounging about inside on tables as they usually did. I opened the door and we walked inside in silence. The air was icy-cold. You could have heard a pin drop.

I shivered a little, found a chair and sat heavily on it. Someone up the back made a joke about trains. No one laughed.

I opened the attendance book. The name of the boy who had died had been crossed out. In thick black texta. A life erased with a permanent marker.

As I was marking the roll, I heard a sharp intake of breath and felt someone move closer to me. I was at the name before the dead boy's. I looked up. A student was trying to get my attention without being obvious about it. I could sense that she was concerned that I didn't know about the boy's death. I tipped my book toward her slightly, so she could see that his name had been crossed out. A look of relief passed over her face. My eyes stung as I fought back tears.

I had no idea what to say. So I said nothing and continued to mark the roll. And then we sat and waited for the bell to ring.

That was it. Nothing more. I had no tricks for this situation either personally or professionally.

I so desperately wanted to do something. Anything. I wonder if I would have used the tricks in my bag if I had been aware of them at the time? It certainly would have been difficult, requiring courage and guts. As it was, I was overcome with shock. I felt completely powerless and useless. If I couldn't even look my students in the eyes, what could I possibly offer in the way of strength or guidance?

Now that it's many years later and I have a bag of tricks (and feel okay about using them, too), it does make me sad that I wasn't able to offer more to those young people around me.

Thankfully, this need has been recognised and there are now whole teams of grief experts who visit schools and communities when grief and loss arise. People like my co-author Kerry Abramowski.

Trick #5 visualise your grief

Sometimes it's easier to understand things when you have an image in your mind. Here is an exercise that may help you to visualise grief and the process of healing.

So, when you took that last corner on your bike way too fast, you skidded and broke your leg...

How did you know that you had broken your leg?

Did you feel pain? Did you know straight away that it was sore? Did you hear the bone snap, or did the pain just appear mysteriously?

What steps did you take to remedy the fracture?

Did you need plaster? Bandages? Did you go to the doctor? A hospital? How did you get there? Who else assisted you?

How long did the fracture take to heal?

A month? Six weeks? Longer? Is it healed now?

What effect did the fracture have on your life?

Were there things that you could no longer do? Did you have to stop playing your favourite sport?

Some things you learned to do with a broken leg were...

Did you try new things? Different ways of kicking a ball? Skiing on one leg?

Some feelings the broken leg (and its mending) aroused in you were...

Can you recall what your feelings were? Were you frustrated? Did you enjoy relying on others for things that became difficult?

Some advice/comments people gave you was/were...

Did you listen to others? Was it helpful? Did you use their ideas?

Okay then, so what does a broken leg teach us (apart from slowing down)? There are quite a few things.

It teaches us that the human body is self-healing. That there is a time frame for healing. That healing can be slow and painful. That the basic starting point is recognising that the leg is broken. That continuing to walk on the broken leg will cause further damage. That you must take care of yourself while your leg is broken and allow the break to heal.

Now, let's look at a broken leg in relation to grief.

1. You can't get to fixing the leg until you know it's broken. You can't get to dealing with your grief until you know it's there.

The starting point is recognition. For you to deal with grief, you need to recognise that it exists.

Once you've recognised that you've broken your leg it will not get better if you continue to walk on it.

Once you've figured out that you're grieving, it will probably get worse if you don't do anything about it. If you deny it or leave it, daily life can become harder to deal with.

2. The human body is amazing. It is self-healing. Your leg will heal with help from medicine, doctors, family, friends and, most importantly, yourself – your spirit, your desire to walk without a limp, to run and to mend.

Your grief too will heal with the assistance of your bag of tricks and the coping strategies it contains.

After any bone breakage, some scarring of bone or tissue will always remain. There will always be some evidence that you had a broken bone, even if it can only be found by x-ray.

It is the same with grief. You will always know.

Changes happen which will be with you for life, and the lessons you learn will serve you for a long time. A scar is the result of a healed wound. Although the pain of the wound will lessen, the scar will always be with you. Your grief, too, will heal over time but a scar will remain.

3. The healing of your leg and your grief may be slow and painful.

You know the saying 'It won't happen overnight but it will happen'? Patience and tricks from your bag are the things that are called for during your healing. Unfortunately though, even these things won't automatically get you through a grieving situation quickly or painlessly.

4. There is a time frame for healing both the leg and your grief.

The amount of time taken will be different for every single person. No one can tell you exactly how long it will be before you will feel better. Just know that you must take as much time as you need to accomplish your healing.

Trick #6 own your grief

Grief is something that has to be owned. It does not just go away if you pretend you can't see it. Of course, you can have breaks from it in those moments when you forget. You have to bring grief into the open so that it does not become a monster that grows by itself.

To own grief you need to speak it or write it. No one else can do this for you because your actions and feelings are your own. When you talk about your inner feelings, you take an important step towards owning your grief.

Speak your grief out loud. For example, 'I am so sad that that stupid boy broke up with me. He doesn't know what he's missing.' Or 'I am really pissed off that I have cancer.' Say it even louder. Shout it to the sky or into your pillow.

Another way is to write your grief. Keep an exercise book beside your bed, in your pocket, in your bag. Whenever the voices in your head switch on, write it down. Write your feelings in a stream of consciousness. Put pen to paper and write without stopping to think or to read what you've written. Write a poem. Or a story. Or a letter.

By owning grief, by acknowledging that it exists, you are preparing yourself for what is to come. You are pushing your boundaries so that you may break through them. You are growing. You are on the verge of a new adventure.

Trick #7 dear diary

Write in a diary as often as you need to. Carry it with you.

Trick #8 not being alone

Do you ever feel like you're on your own? That no one could understand how you feel? (Maybe you don't even fully understand how you feel.) That whatever you say gets misunderstood? That your feelings of sadness or isolation are so big that they consume you? That there is no logic to your thoughts or emotions? That there seems to be no way out?

If you answered yes to any of these questions, then take heart. You are not alone.

Grief makes you feel this way. There are standard grief reactions (see trick #1) – and one of the most common reactions is feeling like you're totally on your own.

Because of all the emotions that come with grieving, it can be difficult to express what's going on inside. Sometimes words are simply inadequate. Not being able to communicate what's happening can make you feel even more alone. It's hard to talk about something when you don't quite know what you want to say. And how do you know who to talk to? Friends? Family?

Sometimes, those closest to you are not equipped to assist with your grief. They may want to be there to help, but don't quite know how. For so many reasons, grief can make you feel alone.

You are not alone.

Knowing that you're not the only one to face a challenging experience can help. Seek out other people who have been through a similar situation. See how they've dealt with the obstacles that confronted them as they walked their path. They might give you some tricks you can add to your bag.

It may also be quite a relief to know that your feelings of wanting to smash plates or burn down the house have been felt by other people too.

Other peoples' stories can show you that it is possible to survive the most difficult situations that life can dish out.

Everyone has a circle of people who they could turn to in a crisis – trusted adults, relatives, teachers, counsellors, youth group leaders. Trick #10 will assist you to work out exactly who you might turn to for help.

One great way to share stories and support is within the safety of a support group. There are squillions of these in every city and some country towns. If you ask a trusted adult you are sure to be pointed in the right direction and will find the appropriate group for you.

Sharing your experiences with others can be both helpful and healing. It certainly shows that you are not alone in your grief.

When I was a boy of fourteen, my father was so ignorant I could hardly stand to have the old man around. But when I got to be twenty-one I was astonished at how much the old man had learned in seven years.

Mark Twain

Trick #9 the ideal support person

My co-author, Kerry, says, 'There is always somebody there. We just have to choose them, and we just have to ask them.' There is always someone. This trick is an old standard. It can have a huge and immediate impact. It works time and again. Take the time to learn it carefully and fully.

Knowing that you're not the only one going through an ordeal doesn't mean that you won't feel like crap sometimes. It's all very well to know that crying into coffee cups is normal, but that knowledge doesn't help you at 3a.m. when you just need someone to be there for you.

It's especially hard to explain what's going on when your feelings are changing so rapidly that even you can't keep up. It may be that in one moment you feel in need of a cuddle. In the very next moment you need a good old belly laugh so you put on your favourite funny film (mine is still *Flying High*). And then you discover that you're weeping in the bit that you always cracked up at. Suddenly you're starving but the only thing you can stomach is stale flat bread, and then you realise that you haven't eaten properly for days. You have a vivid recollection of a really funny conversation and you go to call your friend – but they died a week ago. So you put the telephone receiver down and stare out the window in silence for 30 seconds. Or three hours. It doesn't matter, really.

Is there any one human being who can understand all of these things in another person? Is there any one person who can anticipate your needs and mood even before you do? Who knows when to be quiet, when to speak, when to nod serenely, when to laugh, when to cry, when to look at you, when not to look at you?

Probably not. But that is often what we want and expect of people when we are in a grief situation.

Following is a wish list compiled by a group of young people who were asked what would make an ideal support person:

- Someone who will just listen – who will hear me and won't talk over the top of me
- Someone who doesn't say 'I know how you feel'
- Someone who doesn't judge me
- Someone with a sense of humour
- Someone who won't criticise me or make me feel stupid
- Someone who has had some sort of experience with a loss like mine
- Someone who can relate to me. Someone who can give me good advice
- Someone with lots of tricks up their sleeves
- Someone who will put their arm around me
- Someone who is free and accessible whenever I need them

- Someone who is genuine
- Someone who cares about me

In reality, this would have to be some incredible person. Most of the group of young people agreed that this person doesn't exist in everyday life, in real life.

So they set about discussing the changes that happen during the crisis of grieving. Some interesting things began to emerge. Although it would be a big ask for one person to be all of the amazing things listed above, the discussions revealed that in a crisis situation most people thought that they could be many of these things.

A crisis situation does not last forever. So asking someone to make themselves available to you during a crisis is not like asking them to listen to every problem you will ever have for the rest of your life. A crisis situation is a very intense period, which ends.

If you were to ask yourself, 'In a crisis, could I be all of the things listed above?' probably you could, particularly if you were asked to be these things by someone you care about.

In the group we discovered that most people would want to be asked for their help and to be made aware that they were needed.

If you are grieving, you need to help people to help you. Choose a person with whom you feel comfortable, and approach them with honesty and truth. Most people would be happy to be approached in this way. The majority of people are compassionate and wonderful. They care about other people, and genuinely want to help in whatever way they can.

It is important to remember that the person you have set your sights on may not be superman or superwoman. If they have agreed to help but it's not working out for you, be prepared to try again. And again and again, if need be. In fact, it's often helpful to have a couple of people 'up your sleeve'. This is so that if your first support person does not work out, you won't be left in the lurch.

When you're learning something, like riding a bike, you don't expect to do it perfectly first go. There will be a few grazed knees on the way.

Expressing grief – your innermost needs, fears, thoughts and feelings – also takes skill and is definitely a balancing act. If you lose your balance with the first person you choose, then try again. Be prepared to keep looking until you find the right person. Or people. Sometimes you'll have more than one support.

In among this, you are taking care of yourself as well as letting others take care of you. So long as you remain open and honest about where you are at emotionally, you will find support and comfort when you need it.

Trick #10 adults or friends?

Many adults will be able to provide you with direction, focus, clarity, comfort, nurturing, compassion, sympathy, empathy, a good strong cup of tea and more.

People who are older and who genuinely care about you often have a bit (or a lot) of life experience. They may also surprise you with a good sense of humour. Older people have enough years behind them to have made a few mistakes over time, and to have seen some grief. Adults can be particularly good at juggling emotions, handing around the chocolate biscuits and knowing where the tissue box is. When you need to talk to someone, the adults around you might not be your first choice. But a lot of adults love quiet little nooks and crannies along with cups of tea and things like that. It can be just what the doctor ordered – a quiet chat about where you're at and how you are feeling.

Give the adults around you a go. Be tolerant of them the way they need to be tolerant of you. Accept them the way you need to be accepted by them. If it's possible, talk about things with them. Or write. If you can't talk or write, then pass on a message through a trusted adult. The adults in your life might not remember what it's like to be young. Don't assume that they know how you're feeling or what you're thinking. If you can, let them know.

Your friends and brothers and sisters may also help you along the way. Frequently, friends are in a great position to offer support and encouragement. They can be excellent if you want someone to listen to you in a way that adults just can't. It's great to confide in and share with a friend when you know that you are being heard and understood.

In your grief, it is perfectly okay to use people – people of all ages – in the nicest possible way, of course. If you want some advice on how to cope with, say, crying all the time, then arrange for an adult you trust to be there for you. There will also be times when you only want your friends around. In grief, you are allowed to be selfish for a while.

Call on others as you need them.

Trick #11 resisting judgment

It's so easy to judge yourself. Most people do it on a daily basis – 'My bum looks big in these jeans. I'm taking too long to do this puzzle.' – you know the kind of thing.

Go against the grain and avoid the temptation to judge yourself. Wherever you are and whatever the circumstances, please don't judge your own situation against somebody else's. Every situation is as different and unique as the person experiencing it.

At my own sickest time in hospital, I was wheelchair-bound, bald as a bowling ball, skinny as a rake and I had a halo frame contraption drilled (yes, with screws) into my head at four points. It was not pretty.

So you can only imagine how I felt when other well-meaning patients would come along with massive lumpy foreheads or no legs or three heads, and look at me with pity and say, 'Oh, you poor thing. I'm glad I'm not in your shoes.'

In their eyes I was much worse off than they were. My own perception was that I wasn't all that bad, but as I could only whisper, I mostly missed out on telling them that!

To compare yourself with someone else almost inevitably leads to disappointment. And judgment is unfair – mostly to yourself. So steer clear of comparisons and judgment.

Trick #12 don't snap out of it

It will take time to move through grief. There are no quick fixes. But it can be really hard for others to watch you going through a tough time. To get through grief, though, you have to stay with the hard feelings, so be careful of people's 'snap out of it' phrases.

'Don't worry, it happens to us all.'

'You'll see things differently tomorrow.'

'It's God's way of showing you that you're strong.'

'I know how you feel.'

'You'll feel better in the morning.'

You often hear things like this when people don't know how to deal with a difficult situation. They might feel uncomfortable or simply not know what else to say. Be patient with them. And try to remember not to use phrases like that yourself.

Trick #13 O2

Take some time to smell the roses.

Recently it has come to my attention that the average human being rarely uses their full lung capacity. To breathe. In, out. In, out.

When we breathe good, clean air deeply we can enhance all our vital bodily components and inject a sparkle and a tingle into our beings. And into our immune system.

Breathing is one of the few functions of the physical body that we can consciously control. Deep-sea divers spend hours learning to hold their breath for long periods. Breathing is one of the focal points of meditation. Some cultures even believe that we are born into this life with a certain number of breaths to take, and that once they have all been used up, we die.

Breathing. Oxygen. The elixir of life.

Many respected health professionals acknowledge that the level of oxygen in the blood can have a positive impact on curing disease in the body. Where do we obtain oxygen? Breathing!

The gentle art of breathing.

Back when I was a school teacher and students would become overexcited or agitated, I would suggest that they slow down and take a few deep breaths.

As a performer, in those anxious moments of waiting in the wings or of sitting with fingers poised over the piano keys, it was focused breathing that helped me where nothing else could.

The ocean is therapeutic because of the vast amounts of ozone in the air. The salt and wind and foam spray are enough to raise energy levels and invigorate the mind. Similarly, the bush with its vast array of ozone-giving plant life, along with an almost tangible sense of peace, can be very healing.

To be in nature and to breathe it in deeply is innately healing. Whenever you can, take a gentle stroll along the beach or through the bush, breathing deeply with your conscious awareness.

Or sit in a comfortable chair and close your eyes. Just breathe. After a while you'll notice that air moves through one nostril at a time, and then transfers to the other. If you concentrate, you can feel this air flow in the space above the upper lip. It is possible to become aware of which nostril is working, and when.

Take the time to fully saturate your lungs with air. By focusing inwards and being aware of your lungs, you can expand and oxygenate them to their full potential.

The outbreath, too, has a special importance. You can enhance your vital life-force by breathing out fully. Releasing all the air in your lungs is something that doesn't always happen naturally. As you read this, with your next outbreath, stop breathing and then breathe out again before breathing in.

Take in some slow, even breaths – counting is helpful, up to three at first and then back to one – gradually increasing the number of counts and thus lengthen the amount of time for each breath. Allow yourself to become relaxed in your physical being. Enjoy the sensation of tuning in to your breathing. Notice your heartbeat. And any other movement that is happening on the inside of you.

'Controlled' or 'aware' breathing can be done anywhere – in a bus or in a queue. It's an excellent relaxation technique.

Trick #14 listening to feelings

An English professor at college once told our class about how he dealt with the death of a close friend. He said he went home and played a recording of the saddest music he knew. He plunged into the darkness; he acknowledged his grief and allowed it to pour out. He knew that the only way he could get beyond his loss was to allow himself to feel the pain in all its intensity.

Helen M. Luke

Dealing with feelings in a time of grief is like keeping hundreds of juggling balls in the air, sometimes for weeks or months or years on end. When you're sad you might not feel like clowning around with juggling balls, so here are a few pointers about feelings.

Feelings, like your fingerprints, are unique. Feelings are your very own personal, inner reactions to what is going on around you. Perhaps another person does not experience the same feeling as you. That is to be expected, they are them and you are you.

Respect yourself and your feelings, whether you are angry, sad, happy, joyful, bitter, serene or something else at this moment. Feelings are neither right nor wrong, good nor bad. They simply are.

That doesn't mean though, that they give you the right to behave badly or inappropriately.

Feelings are trying to tell you something important about yourself. They are like yellow traffic lights, which don't say either stop or go. They say, hang on a minute, just slow down. What's going on around you? Have a think about what your choices are and then act appropriately.

Feelings and emotions can encourage you to explore something important which is going on inside you. Feelings keep bugging you until you listen to what they are trying to tell you.

Anger tenses and whitens.

Fear raises your heartbeat.

Fright sends you cold.

Anxiety ties a knot in your stomach.

Hurt tightens your chest.

Embarrassment reddens your face.

Shock makes your body shake and your voice tremble.

Every emotion or feeling causes a physical change in you. By listening to your emotions, you can learn the messages they hold. Even your own body will not allow you to ignore your feelings. It will keep giving you messages until you listen.

Imagine that when you are born, you come complete with your own personal CD which starts off blank. As you move through your life, the CD gets added to. You burn messages onto it from your parents, friends, teachers, and anyone else who has an influence over your life. You absorb and take on all of their ideas about feelings. You learn to deal with your feelings in the same way that they did. If you have learned that feelings and emotions should be ignored it will be harder to deal with grief. If your CD isn't tracking properly and thoughts like 'I can't tell anyone how I feel' or 'I should just ignore my feelings' are playing over and over, then it's time to take action. Switch CDs and burn some tracks that make you feel good – with messages about openness, trust and feeling worthwhile.

It can be difficult to catch hold of and understand your feelings. Here's an exercise which may help. Grab a few pieces of paper and a pen.

Name how you are feeling at this moment. Write it down. For example, 'I feel really annoyed because I was reading this book, and then I had to go and find a piece of paper and now it's like I'm back at school.'

Remember to begin your sentence with 'I feel' or 'I'm feeling'. Include as many feelings as you need to.

Describe what the feeling makes you want to do. For example, 'I'm so angry I just want to throw you out the window.' (That's my five year old son's latest!)

Write down your description.

Put the feeling into pictures or images. 'I'm as happy as a pig in shit.' (You get the picture.)

You don't have to be an artist. Stick figures are okay.

Recall a time in the past where you felt as you do now. 'It's just like when I went to the dentist and had all my teeth ripped out.' Write it down. (You may not have an experience to compare your current feelings with. If you can, pick a past experience that comes close to what you're feeling now.)

Grief makes your feelings so much more difficult to deal with that expressing yourself is vital. You'll be surprised at how much better you feel by getting your feelings out of your head and onto paper. It will also make juggling lots of different feelings easier.

Trick #15 sleep

Sleep whenever you possibly can. It gives your body and mind a fighting chance to deal with another day.

Trick #16 dealing with 'why me?'

'Why me? I don't go around hurting people. I don't throw rubbish out of cars. I'm the best person I can be. Maybe I'm not perfect, but who is? I don't deserve this.'

To ask the question 'why me?' often (but not always) shows that you are in a grief reaction. 'Why me?' Two little words. The simple answer to this question is that there is no simple answer. Sorry. As Kerry says, 'Nine times out of ten there won't be an answer to "why me?"'

Sometimes I think that asking 'why not me?' is closer to the mark. But there is value in questioning, because it helps you – step by step – to build a staircase toward understanding. Each time you ask the question, you open yourself up to the possibility of gaining new insight.

Everyone experiences crisis. People everywhere, of all ages, ask 'why me?' Part of being human is to experience life in all its colours, and that includes grief.

Happily, we do have a choice as to how we will look at or perceive things that happen to us. From the time we are quite young we can make conscious choices about how we view our lives. We can take charge of what we think.

Take my experience, for example. I had quite a few months in hospital where I had very restricted use of my arms and legs, and a vocal cord had been paralysed as the result of surgery (which saved my life). But I couldn't talk. I could only manage a very hoarse whisper.

During this time I became quite despairing of my situation. I was really sad at my dependence on others and my difficulties with talking. I found that some people would not take the time to lean in close to me to hear what I needed to say and others would treat me as though I were stupid. Some people would speak loudly and slowly to me as though to a child, and others would ignore me completely.

Rather than concentrating on the 'why me?' of my awful situation, I really needed to focus on getting well. I had to radically change my perception. I had to involve the 'why not me?'

Over a long time I managed to adjust my perception of my situation, and I found that I could laugh and joke about it (sometimes). A great bonus was that I stopped feeling quite so desperate and angry. In the longer term my voice has become a little louder – though my children think it's hysterically funny if I try to yell at them.

Moving forward: from 'why me?' to 'what now?'

If someone jumps out of a plane with a parachute strapped to their back, they can't turn back. It's too late for them to ask 'why me? Why am I doing this?' as they fall through the sky. There is no point. They must live in the moment. And so, a better question to ask might be 'what now?'

We live in moments of time. Some are fantastic and some are shit-awful. In any given situation, a series of life events have led to this moment. It's vital to live in the moment and deal with whatever arises. If we jump from a plane there is always a small chance that the parachute won't open. But it would be futile to focus our attention on that once we've jumped. Far better to sit back, smile a big fat smile and enjoy the ride. There is no turning back. Forward is the only way to move. It's the same with the process of grief. We cannot move backwards in time and change the events that have led to this point. What we can do is begin to employ some coping strategies or tricks by deciding to deal with the situation in the here and now.

In this way we can assist ourselves. The 'why me?' question cannot be answered. In the long run, it is not so important.

The much more helpful question to ask is 'what now?'. How am I going to deal with this?

Trick #17 finding your way

If you walk up a path that somebody else told you to walk, and you look ahead and you don't like where you're going, and you look back and you don't want to return, step off the path. Pick yourself a brand new road.

Maya Angelou

You can deal with grief in your own way. You don't have to believe what a bunch of other people believe. You can if you want, but you don't have to. What happens next is up to you. Even if it doesn't feel that way at first.

When you are young – *because* you are young – you have the luxury of not quite conforming to rigid rules or patterns of behaviour. In grieving, you are entitled to make full use of this and let it benefit you. You are in a unique place where you can truly discover what makes your heart weep and sing.

Because you are young it's expected that you will explore, learn, grow and make mistakes. Adolescence can be a freer and more liberated space than adulthood.

Why not use this. Open up your eyes and take a look at all the possibilities around you. You are in a great place to question things and explore who you are, your beliefs, your world. You can ask questions and pull apart the answers. You can explore and not be restricted except by the limits of your imagination.

You don't have to take on any of the adult hassles associated with grief. Too often, older people have lost their desire to question and to experiment with ideas. Sometimes they have become set in their beliefs, and then feel burdened when dealing with a situation involving grief and loss. This is where being young is in your favour.

You shouldn't ignore adults. But be aware that one person's grieving method may be totally inappropriate for another. No one should have to deal with being bogged down or depressed by an adult's choice of coping strategies.

When big events happen involving grief and loss most people turn to what they know – whatever this is and as limited as it may be. Usually, it means that you embrace beliefs that you've grown up with. Which is pretty funny really, because sometimes you don't even believe in these ideas, it's just that you're used to them.

For instance, families (the people we grew up with) teach you things that you do not question when you are young. As a child, you generally accept that adults know what they're on about. So, you take on the values, habits and behaviours that come from the people around you.

All families are different. And mostly they are doing the best that they can. Some are happy, some are sad. Some are big, some are small. Some live in mansions, others in shoeboxes. Some families do not touch, hug or kiss. Others have great-aunts who insist on a big fat smooch. Some do not talk about death or people who have died. Some never shut up. Some have secrets. Some don't talk to each other at all.

Families cope in their own unique ways when things go wrong. So as family members, everyone learns their 'family' way of coping. That is, you use your family's bag of tricks. And the ironic thing? Sometimes this bag of tricks doesn't work for you. Sometimes it doesn't even work for anyone.

I am not suggesting that you renounce your religious upbringing, abandon your family and move to a commune to find yourself (although who am I to stop you?). But look inside yourself, and open up to some of the many possibilities that may truly help you with coping and healing.

Keep an open mind. Don't turn your nose up at something because you don't understand it, or because friends and family scoff at it. I had to confront a lot of fear – my own and other people's – in order to use some alternative treatments. It was extremely challenging.

Try new ideas that you find in this book, even if they don't appeal to you at first. Get out of your comfort zone. It's even okay to feel vulnerable or silly. Meet the challenges of your grief head-on.

Trick #18 places to grieve

Under the shower. Walking the dog. Lying in bed. There are some places that are better than others for releasing emotions. If you can help it, it's easier not to have a sobbing session in class, for instance. Or at a concert. Not that there's anything wrong with sobbing.

But if you know that you're feeling a bit vulnerable and sad, then look after yourself by choosing a place where you can cry and not feel that you're being stared at. This might mean that you leave the cinema early, or move into another room away from where there are lots of people. Or you might stay in that room and tell your life story. It's really up to you. Whatever. It's okay.

There may be times when you have no control of your emotions and that's okay too.

Grief is better out than in.

Trick #19 if you don't eat, you die!

Eating is really important. And when you're sad or angry or stressed you sometimes don't eat very well. It is easy to become run down physically when things seem to be falling apart emotionally.

Grieving is a time when you have to look after yourself. You can't let your body get run down, because you need it to work well for you. So, take a little time and ensure that you've got some healthy food in the fridge.

Some of the best foods to eat are the ones that offer immediate nourishment and have an 'alive' quality. Whole grains and fresh fruit and vegies are perfect and contain loads of health-giving properties. Organic fruit and vegies are excellent.

Juicers are fantastic. Stock up on celery, parsley, fresh carrots, beetroot, apples, ginger – anything that is in season and looks appetising. A glass of fresh juice each morning can give you a boost for the rest of the day.

Taking the time to cook a delicious and balanced meal is a nurturing thing to do. As much as your body will love you for it, psychologically it means that you are caring for yourself too. Which is no mean feat when you are dealing with grief.

Avoid overeating anything. Try to maintain a balance, particularly with foods such as sugars, fats, salt and dairy products.

Eat as regularly as you can. Take the time to sit down to eat and really taste your food. Give thanks for it if you want to. If you can, eat quite slowly and chew well – eating slowly aids digestion. When your system is in shock, digestion is one of the first places you'll feel it – the old 'kick in the guts', or the bloated feeling.

Picture the food bringing energy and zest into your body as you eat it. Imagine it to be warming and healing. Enjoy the fact that while your life is in a challenging place at the moment, food can bring you new energy and strength.

If someone else has made you a meal (some household freezers fill up the moment there is a death or illness – friends and relatives always bring casseroles), remember that it was given to you with good intentions, and let this knowledge warm you along with the food.

It's important to eat well so that you get all the vitamins and minerals that you need from your food. If you're not eating properly, maybe you need to visit a health food shop or chemist for suitable supplements to take.

Avoid dependence on fast-food outlets. Although they're convenient you won't do yourself any favours by eating their food constantly. Grab an apple or something fresh instead.

A suggestion was made to me a few years ago – when I didn't want to obsess about food but I did want to eat well. It was to look at your food and see how close it is to its original form – an apple is an apple from the tree to that first juicy bite, but chocolate iced doughnuts don't grow on trees. A lot of manufacturing and processing has made them, so it's best not to eat them all the time.

Be happy about what you eat. Try not to judge your food, or yourself, as being good or bad.

Whatever it is that you are eating, feel its warmth and acknowledge its nurturing properties. Even if it's a chocolate iced doughnut.

Trick #20 finding out

There's an elephant in the room,
It is large and squatting, so it is hard to get around
 it.
Yet we squeeze by with 'How are you' and 'I'm fine.'
And a thousand other forms
Of trivial chatter.
We talk about the weather.
We talk about work.
We talk about everything else–
except the elephant in the room.

Terry Kettering

Finding out might seem like an odd trick to include in your bag, but not being told things you need to know happens more often than it should.

Are you grieving but you don't know why? Know something's going on but you don't know what it is? Adults tiptoeing around each other?

I have to have two hearts now. One for my mum and one for my dad. They're not together now and I'm not together.

Girl, 15

Anna's story

Anna was sick of walking around on eggshells. She knew something was not right between her parents. She was the youngest of three girls. Her two older sisters had both left home. Lucky them. They didn't have to put up with their mother who had become moody and cranky over the past few months, and sometimes didn't get out of her pyjamas all day.

Anna had stopped inviting her friends over because her mum had become so unpredictable. Just last week she had freaked out and screamed abuse at Anna and a friend simply for walking in the front door. It was so embarrassing. Anna had never seen her mother like this and she didn't know what to do. And it didn't look like her mum was getting any better.

Nothing Anna did was good enough, or the right way. Her mother was a tyrant. Anna loved her mum and hated to see her like this. Saddest of all, Anna couldn't remember the last time she had heard her mother laugh. Or even smile.

Her dad was around less and less these days. He used to work away from home a bit, but now he was home less than one week in four. It was probably a good thing because every time her dad came home she heard her parents arguing well into the night. They thought she couldn't hear, but their hissing and spitting of abuse to each other came through the bedroom walls. The walls seemed paper-thin.

Anna wondered if it was her fault.

Poor Anna. It seems like her parents would be unhappy with or without her being around – that's how their lives are at present. But while Anna is living in such a tense and difficult situation at home it is hard for her to get any real sense of perspective.

Anna's quality of life is being dramatically affected by the behaviour of the adults around her. We don't know if this situation is Anna's fault. She will not know either, until she sets out to get some answers.

At this stage Anna can only guess at what is going on between her parents. It could be anything – illness, an affair, money worries, separation, resentment or something completely unrelated.

We are all entitled to have a bad day here and there, to feel a little off. But the bad times between Anna's parents have been going on for months. Anna knows that something is going very wrong for her parents and, consequently, for her.

It is her right to know some of what is going on with her parents so that she can stop feeling responsible about it and move forward with her own life. Anna needs to know enough so that she can deal with her present situation. She already feels guilty and it's very likely that none of this is her fault.

Grief thrives on secrets.

Anna is living among secrets now and they're affecting her day-to-day life. How can she deal with her grief if she doesn't know what she's grieving about?

Sometimes the adults in your life get it wrong.

Sometimes they don't tell you things you should know – maybe about a relationship breakup, an illness or a death, loss of a job, financial stuff or some other situation that affects you deeply and which you have a genuine need to know about.

Maybe they think you're too young, that you won't understand, that you need to be protected from things, or maybe it's just too hard for them. This can be really difficult to deal with for everyone involved. But the bottom line is that if something affects your day-to-day life, then you have a right to be told.

There is little doubt that, mostly, adults mean well. In some situations, it just mightn't even enter their heads that you need to know what's going on. Or, they might be ashamed that they can't pay the bills, or they might want to save you from feelings of pain. But there is no real way of easing someone else's pain. Pain is something that *must* be moved through.

So, how do you deal with this type of situation?

A direct approach is needed – the situation must be dealt with quickly. This might require you to confront the adult who has made a bad decision on your behalf. The longer you leave this, the harder it will become to talk to them.

You need a plan of action and might require the help of a supportive adult – maybe a school counsellor or an older friend. Refer to trick #9 – the ideal support person.

So once you've taken the plunge and decided to confront the situation, what do you say? The most important thing is to speak out your truth. How do you feel about not being told?

By speaking out you are releasing some of the feelings that have built up inside. And you are also giving the adult involved a chance to explain their point of view.

Confrontations can be gut wrenching. It takes a lot of courage to speak your truth, especially when you don't know what the outcome will be.

When you speak out your anger, fear and frustrations, you give yourself the chance to understand. Maybe, just maybe, you'll be able to make sense of the situation. If you're lucky, you might even be able to lay the whole issue to rest.

There is always the chance that you won't like what you hear. Even this is okay. It is better to open something up with truth, than let it eat away at your insides. Whatever the outcome, the fact that you had the courage to speak your truth is a huge step. It is very difficult to do.

Every person has the right to grieve for their losses, and nobody else has the right to decide if or when you may grieve. Remember too, that there are adults who can assist if this feels too big to handle on your own.

Trick #21 punch that bread

Find a bread recipe. Make the mixture. Be patient. Let the yeast rise. Pick up that stretchy gooey wad of dough and PUNCH IT!

Knead it. Roll it. Pummel it. Turn it. Throw it. Knead it some more. Turn it upside down and around. Stretch it. Twist it. Wring it out. Punch it some more. Flex those muscles and sweat a bit. Bake it. Let the smell permeate the kitchen.

Slap on some butter. Share with a friend.

Trick #22 who am I?

The simplest questions are the most profound. Where were you born? Where is your home? Where are you going? What are you doing? Think about these once in a while, and watch your answers change.

Richard Bach

It's really common to question your sense of self. We all do it (maybe a lot more than some of us will admit). Most of us experiment with our sense of who we are. We dress up, dye our hair, hang out with different friends and all sorts of other stuff. From time to time your sense of who you are can become blurred or even disappear completely. This happens as you experiment with life and discover who you do or don't want to be.

But you can also lose your sense of self suddenly as the result of shock or grief, or when situations arise which make you question your deepest levels of being. When you're grieving, it's pretty easy to lose your sense of who you are. Particularly if you've been changing your mind about it anyway.

All sorts of things will make you question yourself, but during grief everything seems bigger because you are in a heightened emotional state.

When something that you know and understand and believe in is shattered, it shifts something very deep inside. It causes confusion, uncertainty and doubt. About who you are. About why you are here. About anything and everything.

For instance, take a relationship break-up. It doesn't have to be a boyfriend/girlfriend thing, but it can be. Just some sort of deep and meaningful friendship that is over, a situation with a sense of loss. There has been a fight and hurtful things have been said. There is no way to take back what has happened, and it seems impossible to fix. It's like being kicked hard in the stomach.

Now, there are several ways this could develop. You could keep fighting and blaming and the situation will go on and on. Guilt and resentment will build and nothing will be fixed.

But if you are clever, you will use this as a springboard and leap into the good things the situation offers. You will look at yourself and the part you have played. You will question your actions. You will gain insights from them. You will take the appropriate action. And along the way a new and stronger sense of self might blossom. So that even though your boy/girl/friendship has suffered, your belief in yourself has not been shattered completely. And, although you might feel like crap, you can gain some wisdom if you ask honest questions of yourself and listen to the answers.

Be mindful of not becoming a victim in this situation. Sometimes it's easier to convince yourself that life is negative, than it is to move on from something.

Kerry once said, 'If you have the courage to look at yourself and can process what you are going through, then you've got the most important thing life will give you. And that thing is choice.'

Choice is a wonderful thing. It is SO empowering. For instance, in the situation above you might choose to forget the friendship/relationship, or you might decide that you want to make it work and apologise – you can choose. In the overall scheme of things, questioning your sense of self can be helpful. It's not about changing who you are, but about getting to know yourself better.

Trick #23 to blob or not to blob

Being physically active when you're grieving creates an important psychological advantage. When you maintain your body through mindful exercise, diet and meditation, you're giving yourself a fighting chance to cope to the best of your abilities.

Personally, I have never been one for strenuous workouts and rigorous 10-kilometre runs. I prefer to keep physically active through things I enjoy. I did join a gym once but spent a lot of time staring out the window at people walking their dogs.

Yoga is great exercise. It's gentle in that you don't have to be sweating all the time for it to work. The stretching you do in yoga is fantastic – it massages the entire body, even the internal organs, and it stimulates the immune and respiratory systems so that they function at their peak.

It is really beneficial to have a set exercise routine. It allows you to work off some of your excess emotion and can even assist you to maintain a degree of balance and equilibrium. Exercise is empowering. If you don't have a daily routine, why not rustle one up now?

Take the dog for a walk a couple of times each day. Or walk around the block. Meet a friend and jog for half an hour. Use your imagination. Dig out your old bike, trampoline or skateboard. Keep playing your team sport.

Whatever exercise strategy you choose, make sure that you give it time to become a regular part of your day. Make sure your half-hour of jumping, hip hop, skipping, yoga, soccer, football, netball remains a priority for you.

Healthy body, healthy mind. Choose something that you enjoy. And just do it!

Trick #24 do we use the word 'dying'?

Kerry and I have had lots of arguments about using the word 'dying'. I have never liked to say that someone is 'dying', because to me it seems like giving up hope. And I believe absolutely that hope and faith can work miracles.

In my life, there was a time when I was literally 'dying'. I wasn't told directly that I was dying. I heard phrases such as 'If she survives, she probably won't walk again'.

If I had been told I was dying, I wonder if it would have caused me to fight harder, or to give up altogether.

Obviously, I didn't die. I was incredibly fortunate and became well again. But the sad fact is that many people who are dying don't get a second chance at life. Kerry believes that we need to be realistic about things. She doesn't believe in beating about the bush. Knowing that someone is dying gives you the opportunity to say goodbye or to do whatever you need to do.

We both knew a young girl who I'll call Bridie. Kerry became particularly close to both Bridie and her boyfriend Pete, who were in their late teens. Bridie had had cancer for several years and was not beating it. She'd had loads of different treatments, and after some time it was obvious to the people around her that she was getting worse, not better. Yet no one ever said the words 'Bridie's dying'. In long illnesses there comes a time when it's appropriate to say things and do things for the last time. Pete and Bridie's emotional investment in one another was huge. They'd been on a long journey together. Pete was feeling really down and he spoke with Kerry one night – according to Kerry, 'Shit happens at night.' Anyway, Pete told Kerry about his confused feelings – his anger at her illness and his tiredness and his frustration. They spoke for hours. The hardest thing for Pete was not knowing. He had no idea whether Bridie would live. Every other time she had been critically ill, she had bounced back for a little while. He just didn't know what might happen. He didn't know what to expect. Finally, very late into this midnight conversation, Kerry spoke the unsaid words out loud: 'Pete, Bridie's probably dying.'

Her words hung in the air for a long time. After an eternity had passed, Pete began to cry. Quite a lot. He said, 'Thanks. No one else has had the guts to say that. I needed to hear it.' Now, Pete was able to take action in a way that he hadn't been able to before. He made the decision to tell Bridie that he loved her. That he had loved her for some time. Which he did.

And she died soon after.

Pete had been paralysed until he heard those words: 'Bridie's probably dying.' Hearing them allowed him to say goodbye in a way that left no unfinished business. So I guess that sometimes we DO need to use the word 'dying'.

Trick #25 what do I say to someone who's dying?

Whatever you need to say. It's as simple and as complex as that.

'I will really miss you.'

'I love you.'

'I am sorry that I've hurt you.'

'Do you know where my black shoes are?'

'Do you want a chip?'

You can say any of these things, even when someone is critically ill.

Sometimes, preparing for someone's death is harder for us than it is for the person who is ill.

Some people live for just a short time after the diagnosis of a life-threatening illness, and others live for many months or even years. Sometimes people are cured of the illness altogether.

As a general rule, you treat people in this situation as normally as possible. Your relationship shouldn't change drastically. If they bug you, then tell them they're bugging you if that's what you'd usually do.

A person with a life-threatening illness does not need to be wrapped in cotton wool or stared at sympathetically with tear-filled eyes. Generally, a person who is ill needs to get about the business of living just like everyone else.

It's really helpful (and not always easy) if we can accept a disease or illness and still see the person underneath. And it's also important to speak about the illness openly and get information, rather than pretending nothing is going on.

Be open, honest and prepared to listen attentively. Incorporate modifications as they are needed. For instance, don't take your friend who's in a wheelchair for a walk along a sandy beach. But as much as you can, behave as usual.

There does come a time when it becomes apparent that a person is preparing to leave this realm, that they are preparing to die. There is often a calmness around a person who is actively dying, and the energy surrounding someone in this situation can be intense and overwhelming. This energy is not something that can be easily described. To speak about it may cause it to seem less than it really is.

Having personally been in a situation where it was appropriate to say goodbye (just before a huge, life-saving operation that there was a good chance I would not recover from), I have had the privilege of experiencing this energy first-hand.

I was not so much aware of what was being said to me, as I was of the energy of the people around me. During this time I sensed a vast amount of love and support from both family and friends, even people who were not physically present in my room.

When people are in this space, it is often enough for a visitor simply to be there. Just to hold your hand or give you a smile. Sometimes it's completely unnecessary to talk, and a visit of a few minutes is all that's needed. Even short visits to a bedside can become incredibly tiring for the person in the bed, not to mention emotionally exhausting for the visitor.

When you visit someone who is unwell, listen to and trust your own intuition. It will tell you when to stop talking or to leave. The person you're visiting will also help you out with clues (spoken or not) as to how they are holding up and whether it's okay for you to hold their hand or stay longer.

Trick #26 the cup – coping on the inside

At some point it may happen that an ill or sad or grieving person will pick you to talk to. You might find yourself thinking, 'What do I say? What do I do? How do I act? Help!' It might come as a surprise to you. It might also be the middle of the night and you're waking life is really busy at the moment.

This sort of work takes strength and courage. Here are a few tips on what to do.

Decide on whether you can be there for this person. If you're okay to talk with them, then relay this to them. Say it a few times and in different ways. You can state the obvious: 'I'm here for you.'

Allow them to talk.

Listen lots.

It's okay to cry (not hysterically) and for them to cry.

Be careful of snap-out-of-it phrases like, 'It'll all be okay', 'Don't worry', 'You'll feel better in the morning', 'Be brave', 'Control yourself ', 'Don't get too morbid', 'Think on the positive side' and many, many more.

Give the person permission to grieve.

If you can, create the right environment – no interruptions, quiet, pleasant, comfortable.

They may be in denial. It's not your job to get them out of it. Leave that one up to a professional and remember that they need to go through their own stages of grief.

Don't forget to just be yourself; after all, that's why you've been chosen to talk to.

After you've been a great listener and done your job really well you'll probably be exhausted and emotionally drained. What you do from here is really important.

Imagine that you're holding a cup when you're with this person. Hold this cup out in front of you. Two hands. Don't drop it. Every single thing that this person tells you goes straight into the cup. Sometimes this cup is huge.

Then, when they have finished talking to you and the cup is full-to-overflowing, take great care to hold onto it. Whatever you do, do not drink from the cup. No matter how thirsty you are. Do not allow their grief, problems, issues, dilemmas or pain to become yours. You have your own to deal with. If you take on theirs too you'll be no good to them and may well become stressed and confused.

Then, as soon as possible, pour out the cup. Talk to someone else who is not so emotionally involved. Then they can pour out their cup to another, and so on.

Empty that cup soon, and then you'll be in a position to hold it out again in future. And by the way, well done if you've had your cup filled. Holding it out to someone is a brave and courageous thing to do.

Trick #27 rearranging

Just move things around.

Eat something different for breakfast.

Rearrange your bedroom or your house. Paint the walls or hang new curtains or exchange your pictures.

Upholster a chair or make some cushions.

Knit a beanbag.

Make a candleholder out of clay. Make a candle out of wax.

Burn some incense.

Bake a cake.

Move the furniture.

Wash the windows.

Shift things about!

Trick #28 saying goodbye

Faith pours from your walls, drowning your calls
I've tried to hear, you're not near
Remembering when I saw your face
shining my way, pure timing
Now I've fallen in deep, slow silent sleep
it's killing me, I'm dying
To put a little sunshine in your life

Badly Drawn Boy

'My mother is probably going to die soon but talk to her about it. I think it will upset her.'

'I have to break up with this guy but I just don't know what to say.'

'Dad's leaving. Mum kicked him out. I'm seeing him tomorrow but I don't know how to act or what to say.'

'They're having a party at school before I leave. I don't even want to go. I'm sick of changing schools.'

'Pixie's being put down tonight after school. She's in so much pain. I know I should go to the vet to pat her while it happens, but I don't know if I can.'

'Mum reckons I should save a lock of hair before it all falls out. It seems really stupid. Shit. I don't want it to fall out.'

'I don't feel all that sad. There must be something wrong with me because I can't cry.'

'My friend is very close to dying. I know I should say goodbye, but how?'

There are so many different situations where we need to say goodbye. Sometimes we even have to say goodbye to intangible things – things we can't physically touch. Things like a holiday that we've really enjoyed, or a job that we're leaving.

Sometimes we need to say goodbye to our ability to do something – for instance, I can't do a backward somersault in the swimming pool any more. It might seem like a stupid thing to grieve for, but boy was I sad about that. Still am!

When it seems that our choices are closing up, it is helpful to focus on what we can do, or look sideways and open ourselves to the other options available.

As Kerry says, 'Goodbye is one way to remove an obstacle, in order to finish the race.'

Sometimes we have the chance to say goodbye to a person who is dying. This can be hard to do, but seize the opportunity – you are fortunate to have it.

Friends have spoken of an immense peace and serenity settling over a person who is actively dying – a peaceful energy which permeates the room and those in it. They have also said that it is something they will never forget.

The words spoken in these goodbyes can really help those who are left behind. To know that you have been a good daughter, son, lover, friend or sibling, and to be told this in the intensely personal presence of a soul preparing to die can provide comfort and healing. A huge amount of healing is possible in these golden moments. It is possible to forgive past wrongs and release anger and resentment. It doesn't always happen this way, but it does sometimes.

The privilege of sharing these last moments with another person is pretty huge. It may seem too huge, too overwhelming. That's okay. There will be things that you need to say and you might kick yourself forever if you don't say them. You will need to muster up all of your courage and strength. Even if the person cannot hear you – they might be asleep or unconscious – you must say what you need to say. For yourself. Why should you do this? As Kerry says, 'It's about no regrets. It's about no unfinished business. No 'what ifs?' or 'I should haves'. If someone you care about died tomorrow, could you honestly say that you have no regrets?'

Having no regrets doesn't just relate to death. It relates to relationship break-ups, friendships, a job or any other situation to which you need to say goodbye. The important thing is to actually say goodbye.

It may be difficult. It may be amazing. It may be upsetting. Again, that's okay. You will survive it. It's crucial to do it.

Lastly, please don't be anxious about talking to someone who is dying. You don't have to prepare a speech. Just say goodbye. Or give them a kiss. Or hold their hand. Or sit with them. Or read to them.

Just be with them. If there's something important you need to say, trust that you will be able to communicate this. All will be well.

If you can gather your courage and seize those moments, they may well become etched into your memory. They become a part of your future self.

Naturally, after such an experience you need time and space for reflection. At this point, it is common to experience a sense of anticlimax.

Plan what you will do after the goodbye, whatever form this takes. You might organise to go for a coffee with a friend. Or you may prefer a walk along the beach, or through the bush. Perhaps you have a special place that you enjoy, or maybe you want to be with your family.

Whatever you decide, plan it beforehand. Imagine assuming that a friend will be around, only to discover they've been whisked away for a surprise trip trekking through Nepal.

Feel what has just happened – do not deny it. And be very proud of yourself.

Trick #29 when you can't say goodbye, release and remember

Sometimes, sadly, you don't get a chance to say goodbye. Sometimes people leave. A parent might leave a family, or a boyfriend leave a girlfriend, or a child leave home, or a friend leave a friendship group, without giving those left behind the opportunity to say goodbye.

Sometimes people or circumstances don't let you say goodbye. Sometimes you forget. Or you might not think that you need to. You might forget to give a kiss goodbye as you head off for the day, or make eye contact as you leave for work.

Sometimes people close to you die unexpectedly. This can be really difficult for those who are left behind, especially if there are conflicts that haven't been resolved.

But you don't always have the chance to say goodbye. The reality of life is that, in most cases, you cannot know when someone will die.

Here now is a story about an unexpected death. It looks at one girl's experience of a friend dying.

Katie's story

Katie and Brett had been good friends forever. As they got into their teens, Brett began to get into trouble for things like theft and stealing cars. He was having loads of hassles at home – his parents didn't have much money and were battling to stay together. His father drank way too much and got violent.

Brett was an only child and Katie was the one person he'd stayed close to. He wanted some support from her. This was becoming really hard for Katie because she was dealing with her own stuff. She had recently been diagnosed with cancer. Her parents were overprotective and she was ill and felt like crap a lot of the time because of the medical treatment she was having. Katie was finding it hard just to stay afloat; she really didn't have extra time or energy to give to Brett. But he didn't seem to understand how exhausted she was.

When she did spend time with Brett, everything was different somehow. When she thought about it, Katie realised that she wasn't having fun with him anymore. He kept demanding her attention. And he did stupid things like trying to get her involved with his crazy schemes for burglary and house-breaking. Did he think she could assault someone with her vomit bag? What planet was he on?

Brett had changed so much that it was hard to be with him anymore. Katie was aware of his home situation but she couldn't do anything about it. He still wanted to hang around but their friendship was becoming really strained. Brett couldn't deal with the fact that Katie was sick – he wouldn't talk about it at all. Couldn't even say the word cancer. It was too painful.

As Brett's life became more and more difficult, Katie's parents stepped in. They liked Brett and knew about his history. They offered him their vacant garage to live in until things settled down at home.

Brett took up their offer but continued his reckless behaviour. Katie's friendship with Brett became both more distant and more volatile. It was hard for them to be friendly with each other except on a very superficial level. They were fighting a lot.

When the knock at the front door came, it was Katie who answered. There were two policemen holding their hats to their chests. Just like in the movies.

There had been an accident in a nearby suburb between a car and a motorbike. The rider had died instantly. It was Brett.

Katie is a teenager who was part of a 'Good Grief ' weekend, run by a teenage cancer support group for patients and their siblings. Katie is a cancer patient in remission, which means that the cancer has left her body.

It had been two years since Brett's death, but the grief was still very raw. Katie felt that no one else had known Brett in the way that she had. Her feelings of guilt were so intense that she shut them out. They were suppressed very deep inside.

During the workshop, Katie was able to share her story in her own words with the rest of the group. There were about 15 of us sitting around on cushions in front of an open fire. After she told her story, we asked questions. In answering these she was able to speak about Brett as she remembered him, without the judgments of others who had known him. For the first time since his death, Katie felt that she had been heard. In the hour and a half that she spoke, without any hesitation or self-consciousness, Katie began to release pent-up feelings that had been with her for years. The bonus in this situation was that there were 15 people to support her in different ways. Fifteen people to assist her in little ways through the guilt she was feeling. And 15 people who didn't think that she was to blame for Brett's death.

Through sharing her story, Katie was communicating at a level that she hadn't been able to before. She was able to open a door inside herself that had been locked. And in opening this door, in identifying that she had been carrying this grief around with her, she was able to take a small step towards healing.

Katie still has a lot of work to do. She will miss Brett whenever she thinks of him, which will be for the rest of her life. And she will probably still feel guilt from time to time.

But now she has a bag of tricks to pull out. She has taken one small step in the process of dealing with grief. And a giant leap forward in her own healing and subsequent growth.

Katie used this weekend to say goodbye. In a sense, the process was a ritual for releasing and remembering.

Saying goodbye doesn't finish the grief process, but it stops Katie from being stuck and allows her to move through some of the other pain she feels.

Not everyone has a weekend workshop to attend (or 15 people hanging about in their lounge room waiting to listen to them). Speaking about someone who has died or left unexpectedly – about the times you've shared, the ways in which they pissed you off, their brilliant sense of humour, what you miss the most about them, and so on – can be an effective way of releasing them, of saying goodbye.

This doesn't have to be done in a group situation. You may be more comfortable speaking to just one person. It could be someone you know well, or you may find it easier to talk to someone you don't know, like a counsellor or other trusted adult.

Trick #30 rituals close to home

What the caterpillar calls the end of the world, the master calls a butterfly.

Richard Bach

There are a variety of things you can do to say goodbye, to help with resolving emotions. Ritual plays a big part in this process. Rituals can give you comfort and ease. They can be simple things like setting the table and sitting down for a meal with others, or getting dressed in your team's colours to go to the footy.

A very simple way to say goodbye through a ritual is to offer up a light-filled thought each morning or evening – some people call this prayer, but you don't have to be religious to do it. This goodbye may take the form of a thought in a quiet moment, lighting a candle at the same time each day, or dropping a pebble into a river or body of water. It might be making a little altar from beautiful flowers, bark and twigs around your home. Or it may be going for a walk along the beach or through the bush.

Sometimes, you might need to do more than these simpler things to complete a cycle and release the intense feelings inside you. You might like to do some of the following.

- Write a letter. You don't have to post it.
- Create a poem in the person's memory.
- Make a picture or other inspired artwork using colours and materials which reflect your perception of that person.
- Create a photo board or collage with your favourite pictures. Make a video clip if you have lots of old home movies lying around.
- Compose a song.
- Gather some friends to scatter flowers and petals over water or fresh grass.
- Plant a tree that will flourish in the climate you're in. Put it in a pot if you think you may move one day.
- Plant a garden – it only needs to be a little one – with a lovely comfortable sitting place where you can be alone.
- Take some time out each day to rebalance your energy and tune in to life by sitting quietly with yourself.
- Have a farewell feast and drink with friends. Those who want to can share a memory with the rest of the group. Light a candle at the table.
- Make a scrapbook of magnificent memories. Paste in photos, writing, clippings, anything that is relevant.

A guy called Kenneth Doka identified four 'classic' rituals that we can use to assist with grief and moving on. They may give you some idea of really nice ways to heal an area in your life, to maintain a tradition, or even to start a tradition!

Rituals of continuity

Say, for example, a friend has moved interstate and you wish to maintain contact. It may be that every month on a certain day, one of you will telephone the other. Or that you will exchange letters. Your own ritual of continuity might involve meeting each other once a year in a certain place. Or it might be as simple as you writing a journal entry or a poem. The ritual of continuity involves a continuing bond with the person or life situation that has been 'lost'.

Rituals of transition

These rituals mark a passage from one phase to another. If a relationship has broken up, for instance, your ritual of transition might involve moving your personal possessions. Or it might involve changing how you look with a haircut or new clothes. In the case of a death, a funeral becomes a ritual of transition.

Rituals of reconciliation

These rituals are designed to finish unfinished business. Yours may involve something quite simple like writing a note to someone to allow for acceptance or forgiveness. Or saying goodbye with an object and a thought – throwing a flower into the water and reading a passage of verse, in order to say goodbye or I'm sorry or I forgive you, when you haven't been able to do so in person.

In the story of Katie and Brett (trick #29), a ritual of reconciliation occurred for Katie because she was able to say goodbye through sharing her feelings. This sharing was significant and allowed for her to move on from the place where she was stuck.

Rituals of affirmation

These sorts of rituals offer thanks for a relationship or situation. They will often complement rituals of reconciliation. For you, it might involve lighting a candle for someone on a special anniversary, or celebrating the change of seasons. The ritual of Thanksgiving in America is one where the whole country celebrates a ritual of affirmation – they give thanks for what they have (and I think they all get a day off too!).

Most rituals are usually accompanied by objects of significance, such as candles, pictures, writing, or natural objects such as stones, shells and feathers.

The thing that separates rituals from other actions is the thoughts or intent behind them. We could throw a flower into the water and think or say out loud 'By throwing this flower into the water, I wish my friend joy and love and light and peace. Goodbye.'

Or, we could simply toss a flower into the water.

Which action is the more significant?

Ritual can be an intense and profound way to release and remember, and it is certainly a trick to consider using for a variety of situations.

Releasing and remembering will happen if you allow them to happen. Kerry organised rituals of remembering as a way for young people to remember friends and family and other things important to them. Lighting a huge bonfire and releasing balloons with messages were two of the activities in the ritual.

Sometimes, in the midst of your grief it's possible to enjoy yourself. Sometimes in performing these rituals, (and sometimes at other moments, too) you may discover that you are actually feeling happy.

If this does occur, allow that good time or happy feeling to stay with you. Try not to judge it, but accept it for the gift that it is. Kerry says, 'It's important to feel good sometimes too, to remember and smile. Just because you are having a good time doesn't mean that you are negating your grief.'

Trick #31 spying on rituals in other cultures

The funeral is the Western ritual for death. Other cultures have pretty amazing rituals. Check these out:

The ancient Egyptians felt that death in one world was the beginning of life in another world.

The ancient Greeks believed that when a person died, his or her vital breath left the body to enter the place of Hades, the king of the dead.

Back in ancient China, it was believed that the dead were reincarnated – either into humans again, or animals such as dogs and pigs, depending on how well they had behaved in this life.

In the South Pacific it was the custom to place the body in a canoe and launch it on the water.

On the anniversary of a death, Roman Catholics offer a memorial mass; Eastern Orthodox believers hold a memorial service; Jews recite a special prayer; and Muslims read a portion of the Koran.

There is a Hindu ritual in which the favourite meal of the deceased is cooked, brought to the temple and served to the priest.

In some Buddhist societies, people burn special counterfeit money, known as 'ghost money' to repay the dead for their kindness.

In Vietnam along the Mekong River, there is a shrine in every home with pictures of the dead. There is a sense that the veil between this world and the next is very thin.

For Australian Warramungas, the etiquette of mourning requires the men to gash their thighs with deep wounds.

Among the Bwende of Central Africa, the obligation to cry may last so long that women have been known to go blind from the constant weeping.

The Dogon of Mali, once they have performed funeral rituals for an absent man, will refuse to recognise him if he happens to return alive.

The Javanese are said to show a lack of hysteria about corpses due to a belief that the dead provide the living with a lesson in being aloof.

The Merina in Madagascar take the bodies out of tombs to dance and talk with them, and to show them recent changes in the area before returning them to their tombs.

A mixed Buddhist-Taoist religion in China used to preserve celebrated priests, sometimes by lacquering the body with gold. The priests would be expected to cooperate in reducing the amount of work required, by fasting before death so as to dry out the body.

The Mbuti pygmies in Africa refuse to acknowledge the dead, and it is forbidden to speak their names.

For the Jivaro, the rotting of the body allows reuse by the living of the dead person's face, identity and name.

In the Lower Congo, the body of a Bwende VIP (very important person) would be turned and smoked over a low fire. When dry, perhaps a year later, it would be wrapped in mats and cloths, creating a figure three times its original size. It would then be buried upright with several slaves pinned down underneath it who were buried alive.

The Aztecs viewed birth and death as being inextricably linked and refused to view death as a finality, choosing instead to focus on the opportunities for new beginnings.

In Mexico they celebrate All Souls Day – The Day of the Dead. This is a time for remembering the dead as well as honouring the continuity of life. The spirits of the departed are believed to return to their homes to visit with families and friends. It is a social and festive time – there are visits to graves, ancestral stories, feasts, dancing, poetry and the creation of elaborately decorated altars. These celebrations look humourously upon death and warmly welcome visits from spirits of the departed.

The plans of a London art critic for the disposal of his remains: his ashes are to be mixed with bread-crumbs and scattered on the steps of the National Gallery, there to be reprocessed by pigeons as 'action painting'.

Something for everyone.

Trick #32 what do I do at a funeral?

When tears come, I breathe deeply and rest. I know I am swimming in a hallowed stream where many have gone before. I am not alone, crazy, or having a nervous breakdown ... My heart is at work. My soul is awake.

Mary Margaret Funk

What am I supposed to wear?
Does it have to be black?
What if I break down and cry?
Do I have to talk to the family?
Am I meant to bring flowers?
How should I act?
Where should I sit?
Am I meant to arrive on time or a bit early?
What happens during the funeral?
I don't want to see the body – do I have to?
And so on.

If you stumble upon a funeral in the street in some African countries, you join in. You dance and sing and eat and drink with many others. Young and old alike are part of the occasion, the procession, the celebration and the mourning. The Irish whoop it up with a wake. In Israel it's done with wailing. Many cultures mark grief and loss with feasts, celebrations, chanting, rituals and meditation. They take time to grieve and they have processes to help them grieve.

Many of us have little idea of what goes on at a funeral, because we don't celebrate the ritual of death with the same energy that we put into other important events in our lives. Most of us would not invite ourselves over for a celebratory funeral drink – but we might feel comfortable to have a drink at a Christmas or New Year's celebration.

We often don't celebrate a life and death by gathering the generations together as other cultures do. Children are often shielded from the entire experience of death. It is interesting that we often protect children from the 'reality' of death with displays of self-control and hushed conversations. Children are far more aware than we give them credit for. By the time my eldest son was two, he had attended more funerals in his short lifetime than birthday parties. He sensed the sadness and enjoyed the chocolate biscuits! Thankfully, now the birthdays are winning.

There is a tendency in our busy world to leave funeral arrangements to the 'experts' – funeral homes – and perhaps just to provide a lovely piece of music or poem to be read out at the ceremony. Usually a funeral happens within a week of the death, so the family are often still in a state of shock and are in no position to make difficult decisions at all.

A friend of mine whose father died had never been to a funeral before. My friend was in his mid-20s and had no idea of what to expect in the days following his father's death. His initial reaction was one of alarm, which quickly turned into feeling overwhelmed when the family home started to fill up with family and friends. He was coping with his own emotions and really had no idea of what to say to visitors. So he escaped. He went to the driving range and belted hundreds of golf balls.

Over the past decade I've been to many funerals. Some of the best have been planned in detail by the family and friends of the person who has died. They have been intensely personal and very reflective of that person. It is particularly wonderful when people are courageous enough to stand up and speak from the heart.

There does seem to be a standard format for funerals, particularly those run by churches or funeral homes. Basically what happens is this—a funeral is held from three to seven days after the death depending on the religion and wishes of the family.

The funeral arrangements are usually made by the family. If you are part of a family arranging a funeral, please take some time to think about what you want to have happen at the funeral.

It is easy to be swayed at a time of immense sadness into doing things like spending more money than you have. You are entitled to arrange a funeral service to suit your budget. Sometimes there are costs at a death that you cannot possibly anticipate.

I heard a beautiful story about a family buying an inexpensive coffin for a grandparent, and the 12 grandchildren each painting on it. It brought the family together before the funeral in a creative way, allowed the children to express their own feelings, and was a very personal goodbye.

Sometimes, there is a separate, smaller service or a 'viewing' before the funeral itself. Viewings are where the person who has died is layed out, usually in their coffin, for friends and relatives to visit. Attending a viewing can be the very best thing you do, or it can be the most traumatic. Think and talk seriously about whether you will attend a viewing.

Kerry's first experience of a viewing was a very powerful one. She had no idea of what to expect and was very apprehensive. She did, however, need to say goodbye to this person who she had loved. To see her friend lying in her coffin, looking beautiful and as if she were just asleep, was not easy to say the least.

But it was an important exercise in accepting the reality of the death. Kerry understood that although the body was there, the soul was on a journey to places unknown. And she was able to say things out loud and to her friend. Things which needed to be said. 'I loved you ... I'm sorry for ... I'll miss you ... I won't forget you.' It was a very important first step in moving on and reconciliation. It was a private and special time.

You can attend a viewing on your own or with someone else. Make sure that you have a plan of action for afterwards – don't wander aimlessly unless it's in your plan. You may need to be with a trusted friend and be supported and nurtured for a while.

If you can, do it. Don't feel bad if you don't. It's not for everyone.

Generally, there is music at the actual ceremony. Sometimes it's religious and at other times it may be reflective of the person who has died. It might be prerecorded or it might be live. Often you will be asked to sing and pray. Usually, there are readings of verses or poems.

One of the loveliest things at a funeral is to hear personal stories or anecdotes from friends and family. Often they are the highlight and can bring some welcome laughter to a solemn occasion. If there is an offer for people to speak to the gathering and you want to talk, go for it. Don't let fear stop you (or the microphone). It is these shared stories that are cherished by all present, often for years to come.

After the service, the coffin will be carried to a waiting car. This is a chance to speak with others who have attended the funeral.

The body will be transported to the cemetery or crematorium – a procession of cars follows and you drive slowly with your headlights on. There may be more verses or prayers while the coffin is lowered into the grave or placed into the fire (at the crematorium). Either of these can be very traumatic. It may be at this time that the finality of death can hit home. Often this is when the tears start flowing if they haven't already. Don't forget to stuff your pocket or bag with tissues even if you don't think you'll cry. Use others around you for support if you need to, and give them support.

After this, people usually gather at a house or church or pub to have some food and drink together. Then they go their separate ways.

Do

- Wear clothes that you feel comfortable in. They don't have to be black, but you might feel conspicuous in your fluorescent T-shirt and luminous platform sandals. If in doubt, lean towards conservative. (Only if you want to.)
- Pay your respects to the family if you can. If you really don't know what to say (and it can be very difficult), a simple phrase such as 'I'm sorry' with a smile, handshake, hug or kiss will usually suffice.
- Take a pocketful of clean tissues.
- Bring flowers, rose petals, a single flower, a shell or something else appropriate. In the case of a death from illness, donations to an organisation are sometimes requested instead of flowers. I like

to bring a sprig of the herb rosemary (which stands for remembering).

- Arrive a little before the scheduled starting time.

Don't

- Be afraid to share your grief or to talk with others, even with people you don't know.
- Be afraid to cry and be open with your feelings.

Attending a funeral can be a very daunting prospect. It can also be a wonderful release and a way to say goodbye. Whether it happens in a church, community hall, a park or a lounge room, a funeral is an essential step in the process of grieving.

Trick #33 turn the radio up

I've lost count of the number of times I wake up to a certain song on the radio (usually one that annoys me) and then I can't get it out of my head! Music is an immensely powerful medium for evoking emotion and for healing.

Music touches everyone. One good, funky song will make a dance floor go off. We hear music at weddings, birthdays, funerals and parties. Most homes have music, or the potential for it, everywhere. Your favourite songs are indispensable when it comes to getting from point A to point B. Travellers on buses, trains, trams, bicycles – even pedestrians and sweaty joggers – will have music pumping to their ears through headphones.

Whether it's digging out your parents' Bob Dylan tribute, or cranking up the bass on your loudest techno compilation – music can be healing. In times of stress and grief, your energy becomes unbalanced. Music has the capacity to rebalance you. Listening to music can transport you to a different mindscape. If you don't play it yourself, or compose it or write it, it still touches you. When you're sad, a piece of music can reduce you to tears. When you want to remember, you can play a song that will transport you to another place and time.

Listen to your favourite songs. Whatever does it for you. If you've never listened to gentle music, give it a go. If someone is sick or has recently died, it can be healing and calming to play soothing music and light a candle. This allows space to breath, and space for thought, memory and focus. Music feeds the soul and energises the brain. Mozart started composing at just three years old, and even now (hundreds of years on) experts say his music is powerful and healing and energised.

It may not be the coolest thing in the world to listen to classical music, lapping waves and gentle breezes, but, hey, in the words of the late great Beatle, John Lennon, 'Whatever gets you through the night...'

Trick #34 turn it down

The quieter you become, the more you can hear.

Baba Ram Dass

With so much noise humming around you, one of the kindest things you can do for yourself is be selective about what you listen to.

The world is loud! When you visit a shopping centre, the noise is an inundation. Music slinks its way through supermarket speakers. It's in elevators and bathrooms, in change rooms and on shop floors. Music lurks in corridors and passageways, and seeps into the very pores of your being.

You might love the wall of music that hits you at the shopping centre. You might even like elevator music. Or having the TV or radio on all the time. Or it might drive you crazy. If you hate it, that's not a good space to be in for healing.

Be aware of how much music and noise there is around that you don't actively choose to listen to. Be selective about what you do listen to.

Turn the TV and radio off if they're just background noise. Listen to music that will help you through your grief. Be quiet sometimes.

Trick #35 I see you baby, shaking that ass

Dance your ass off.

Trick #36 gorgeous skin

Skin is your body's biggest organ. It can become sad and tired when you are stressed. If you are prone to blackheads, acne, cysts or anything else, now is the time to take extra special care.

Choose a bowl and your own small towel just for your face.

You'll need five or 10 minutes to do this. Sit in a comfortable chair and make sure you're warm enough.

Morning: Fill your bowl with warm water and one to two drops of lemon essential oil (not lemon juice – the citric acid might harm your skin). Soak your towel in this water. Fold it in half. Gently press the warm towel onto your face, letting the steam seep into your pores. Press across your forehead, then over your eyes (gently), your cheeks and nose, and mouth and chin. Resoak the towel with warm steamy water, if you need to. Pressing on the facial skin will stimulate your lymph glands to release toxins from the body.

Evening: Fill your bowl with warm water and lavender essential oil, and soak your towel. Repeat the morning's procedure with a pressing motion, and breathe deeply.

Drink water during the day. It feeds your skin like nothing else. Look after your skin.

Trick #37 releasing guilt and regret

Praise and blame, gain and loss, pleasure and sorrow come and go like the wind. To be happy, rest like a giant tree in the midst of them all.

Buddha

One of my first memories of guilt goes back to Grade One in primary school. I kicked Timothy Rolfe in the shin as we lined up to go into our classroom. With my innate five-year-old's wisdom I had reasoned that because he was a boy, it would not hurt him. (I grew up in a house full of girls.) Was I surprised when he kicked me straight back! And it hurt. A lot.

Something in my brain (and my shin) clicked over in a split second and I knew that I shouldn't have kicked him in the first place. Somewhere, in the recesses of my mind, a tangible and raw guilt experience was being born. Sorry Tim!

As with all aspects of life (not just in a grief situation), you can learn from things you wish you hadn't done, or things you wish you'd done differently. If you are feeling guilt, it means that you have a conscience and are 'stuck'. It will be difficult to feel your pain or begin to move through your grief until you get rid of the feeling of guilt. Guilt is an obstacle on the road to healing – like the goodbye that hasn't been said – until it is dealt with.

You experience guilt because things are not as you want them to be. Your feelings of guilt are confronting. They cause you to challenge the way you look at yourself, and sometimes they require you to question your long-term beliefs. For instance, you might be part of a group that picks on another person just for a laugh. Maybe there is a hilarious running joke that you're all in on. But then one day the person you've been picking on snaps, breaks down in tears or lashes out in anger. And you know you've overstepped the mark. You experience guilt.

It is these awful feelings of guilt that poke at your conscience. When you experience guilt, it is important to look honestly at the possible reasons behind it. One of the best ways to do this is to speak it out.

Sometimes, when you want to talk about your feelings of guilt, you're met with phrases like, 'You shouldn't feel guilty', 'Just look at so and so, they really have something to feel guilty over', 'Cheer up, it's not that bad'.

There are lots of other little gems like this. These comments are obviously meant to comfort you, but they can sometimes drive your guilt deeper inside, so that it's even harder to talk about.

It's normal to feel guilt and regret after a loss. It doesn't happen every time, but it's normal. Any kind of loss that stops you in your tracks has a profound effect at a deep level.

You must speak out your feelings of guilt. If you don't, they can affect your day-to-day behaviour. Often the bully in the playground, or the obsessive cake baker, is a person who has not confronted their guilt.

You can cause long-term damage to your emotional and physical health when you run away from your feelings. Some people hide from guilt and regret by pretending they don't exist. There are many ways to do this – through drugs or alcohol, or by becoming insanely busy. But you can't run away from yourself forever. Health comes from learning what your guilty feelings are trying to tell you about yourself.

If you are experiencing guilt or regret that won't go away, deal with it by releasing it. Cooperate with it, but don't let it take over! Look at it. Turn it inside out and upside down. And around. And then look at it some more. Speak about it. The guilt that you are feeling is seeking to bring healing into your life. How? By asking yourself this, by allowing yourself to feel the feeling of guilt, you've taken a step toward releasing it.

To look honestly and openly into your heart is hard, especially when you're sad and hurting. By co-operating with feelings, and moving them along as quickly as possible, you allow healing to begin. Release these totally unhelpful feelings as soon as you can.

Renounce useless guilt–
Don't make a cult of suffering.

Live in the now, or at least in the soon.
Always do the things you fear the most,
Courage is an acquired taste, like caviar.
Trust all joy.

Erica Jong

Trick #38 saying sorry

Forgetting to feed the neighbour's cat. Making an unkind remark. Running over someone's foot. Hurting a person's feelings.

We all need to say sorry now and then. The important thing about it is to understand why you need to say it. You need to know what it is you've done so that you won't repeat it. Have you hurt someone? How?

You can't grow or make peace with yourself without identifying the reason for your apology. It's not enough just to say sorry. You have to truly mean it.

How do you say sorry?

With words. A face-to-face meeting. Or a telephone call. If you need to say sorry and can't do it in person, write a letter or poem. Even if you don't send it, your intent to say sorry is powerful in itself.

With actions. Make amends if you can. Put a situation right if it's within your power to do so.

If you can't fix a situation, talk about how it can be made easier to deal with.

With a gesture. An act of kindness. Mow the lawn for someone who can't do it themselves. Create a gift that you've put thought and effort into. Clean up without being asked. Be thoughtful and considerate.

Use a ritual of reconciliation. Throw a flower into the ocean with the intent of saying sorry. Read a passage from a book or a verse that resonates with you.

Trick #39 drumming out anger

Anger can sit deeply inside. You might blame others, but anger is yours, and yours alone to deal with.

Make yourself a drum kit out of old pots, pans, flowerpots, cooking trays, real drums, or anything else that will make a bloody big noise. Find some drumsticks. Metal on metal works well.

Close the windows and doors. Let anyone at home know what they're in for so they have the option of leaving. Make sure pets are well away and have a further escape route.

Think about where your anger begins. Drum your anger. Often anger starts small, so drum small to begin with. Let it grow. Let it become a huge noise. Let it rise and fall, grow and decline.

Drum until you can feel it in every fibre of your Anger can sit deeply inside. You might blame others, but anger is yours, and yours alone to deal with.

Look at the anger inside. Question the anger inside. Why has it taken hold? Is it time to release it?

Trick #40 releasing anger

Mad, hurt, nervous, grumpy. I want to smash, smash people. I wish that my father loved me now that my mother's gone.

Boy, 16

There are lots of things you can do to release anger. Drumming is one. Breaking or smashing plates is another. So is going for a long run, or another strenuous physical workout. Chopping wood is good. Screaming into a pillow can help. Any of these things might just work. For a while.

Chances are, though, that your anger will return. So you need to find out why you are angry. What or where does your anger stem from? Anger needs to be acknowledged and then removed, before it hurts you or someone else.

You have to unwrap an onion layer by layer before you get to its inside. Anger is like that. Lots of layers of skin. And an inside which sometimes makes you cry. Here's an example of this unwrapping.

Jim's story

Friend: Why is it that you're angry with your father, Jim?

Jim: I dunno. He never really looked after us properly.

How did that make you feel?

Pissed off.

Did your sister feel the same way?

I don't know. Is this meant to be about her or me?

Well, you did bring her up so I thought–

Bullshit. I didn't bring her up. You brought her up just then.

Did I?

Look. I'm sick of this.

Okay, okay. Sorry if I upset you. But you did sort of mention your sister when you said that your father never really looked after 'us' properly.

Oh. I s'pose I did.

Would you have liked your father to be around more when you were younger?

Nuh.

Tell me about him.

He was always drunk. Pissed. Off his head. It was easier when he wasn't there.

Why's that?

Are you thick or something? How would you like having to look after your pissed stinking father and the house and your little sister when you're only nine years old? No. I didn't want him around more. He was no fun to be around.

(The outer skin of the onion has come off. Jim has unwrapped a layer of anger – his father was an alcoholic.)

You said before that you feel angry, Jim. Is that because of your father's alcoholism?

Yeah. It's because of my father's alcoholism.
It sounds like you had a pretty tough childhood.
Yeah.
Tell me about it.
Nothing to tell. Pissed old man flaked out on the bed upstairs when he wasn't in the gutter. That's it.
And your sister?
I looked after her mostly. We did everything for ourselves. Ate toast a lot.
Were you angry that your father didn't look after you?
What do you reckon? Of course I was. I couldn't bring friends over, I couldn't do anything normal kids did. Cos of him. My sister and me, we were like laughed at and stuff.
It sounds like you had a lot of responsibilities at a young age.
Yeah. And he had no idea. Snoring and stinking on the bed. I just wish, just once even, that he would have stopped drinking. For us. His own kids. He just didn't care.
(And more layers have been peeled away. Jim felt unimportant to his father, and unappreciated. He wanted him to be different.)
You said that you had to look after your sister a lot.
Yeah, that's right.
How did that make you feel?
I dunno.
Did you resent having to look after her?

What are you getting at?

Nothing. I'm not getting at anything. I just think it must have been really hard to shoulder that responsibility.

I did alright.

Yes, you did do alright. But I can see that you're obviously agitated at the question.

Nup.

Is there something you want to tell me?

Nup.

So you were okay about looking after your sister, even though it should have been your father's responsibility to do that.

Yeah.

And there's nothing else to tell.

Nup.

Right.

(Silence.)

I believe your sister had a cat.

Yep.

Did you like it?

(Silence.)

Did you enjoy having a cat around the house?

(Silence.)

Or was it just something else you had to be responsible for?

It was alright.

Did you look after it too?

Not well enough.

What do you mean, not well enough?

Didn't talk to me for three days.

What are you talking about?

Three days. Didn't talk. Just sat on the couch.

Your father? Are you talking about your father?

Nup.

Your sister?

(Jim nods, fighting back tears.)

What happened, Jim? Did something happen to the cat?

(Jim nods again.)

Did you feel responsible for it?

I didn't feel responsible. I was responsible. I killed it. It got out the window that I left open, and it was hit by a car.

Jim, you didn't kill the cat.

I left the window open. To get rid of the stink from dad's room. It was a warm night, and I didn't shut the window. I left it open, and the cat got killed.

And now we've reached the inside of the onion, the place from where Jim's anger grew.

Through peeling back the layers of Jim's answers, his friend was able to finally get Jim to talk about why he was angry. Anger brings up a lot of questions. You can feel angry and not know why. The way to unwrap the 'anger' onion is to ask 'why?'. Over and over again if you have to. Just as Jim's friend did. Why? Why? Why?

It would have been easy to assume that because Jim's father was an alcoholic, his anger stemmed from there. In part, it did. But the reality was that Jim was angry on many levels. Along with the drinking, he was also angry with his father for his lack of care, for his irresponsibility, for his selfishness and for not looking after his children. Jim was also angry with the repercussions of his father's drinking. And, deep down inside, he was angry with himself.

Through the peeling back of layers – by asking 'why?' repeatedly – he was able to open the onion (his anger) to its middle, its core.

To release anger, you need to unwrap the onion.

You must ask yourself question after question, just as Jim's friend did. When you're very young, you do this naturally.

My daughter Tahli Rose at four: Why were you late, Nonna?

Nonna: Because I got held up at the shops.

Tahli Rose: Why was someone lifting you up?

Nonna: They weren't lifting me. It's something I say when it means I've had to wait.

Tahli Rose: Why did you have to wait?

Nonna: I had to wait because the person before me was taking a long time.

Tahli Rose: Why were they?

And so on and so on.

Children have an astounding capacity to keep up the 'why?' question, often to the point of their listener's exhaustion. When they get angry, they release it quickly (mostly in the middle of the crowded supermarket by sitting on the floor and screaming for an ice-cream).

As you grow out of childhood, you are required to find other ways to express anger. Sometimes you don't express it – you bury it inside.

To find out why you are angry – to unwrap your own onion – you must look openly and honestly at why you are reacting in a certain way. Don't worry that you won't know when you've reached the core of your anger – it will be quite obvious. You might have a 'light-bulb moment' of realisation, or you could be shocked or thrown for a six. There is a physical gut reaction when you innately know a truth, and it can be very confronting to stand in this degree of honesty. It makes you vulnerable and it might go against everything you've ever believed.

Unwrapping your anger is hard work. Sometimes what you discover isn't pretty.

Other temptations, such as wanting to blame, take revenge, or wallow in guilt, must be overcome quickly. They won't help you overcome anger; they'll just prolong it or divert it into another unhealthy emotion.

Unreleased anger can be like a volcano. A slow burning inside leads in time to an eruption which burns yourself and others. Get to the core of your anger.

Trick #41 artful fun – exploring art

When I think of art as a means of healing, perfect drawings don't spring to mind; precise landscapes or rigid vases full of flowers standing to attention.

I imagine big blobs of colour running into each other on huge, messy sheets of paper lying about on the ground and blowing in the wind. And I also picture people covered in paint, standing back with wide smiles to admire their work.

A while back I ran an art workshop, 'Adventure with Colour', with young people who are living with cancer. We went away for a series of weekends to play with colour and explore the emotions this released.

On the first weekend, we leapt right in at the deep end. Being confronted with a huge expanse of white paper can be very daunting, but we rolled out a few hundred metres of it – it even stretched across a road – got out the buckets of water, paint and brushes, and started.

Within two hours the entire length of paper was covered with paint. Two hundred whole metres. And a few participants would certainly have kept right on painting if there had been more surface to paint on. The work belonged to everyone, including the rain, wind and wombats who walked over it while it was drying.

By beginning with the biggest task imaginable, our budding artists were then able to accomplish anything. A smaller, square or rectangular sheet of paper became very easy to paint on after that.

These young people experienced success very quickly and intensely, and at the conclusion of the workshops we were able to frame and sell dozens of their pictures.

Art has the power to draw out both emotions and creativity at the same time. Due to these extraordinary qualities it becomes a unique means of expression and a powerful tool for release.

It is possible to paint out anger, frustration, rage, fear, helplessness, sadness, bitterness and other such emotions, even with a single colour. Likewise, happier emotions such as joy, love, gratitude, freedom and liberation.

Put on your oldest clothes, whack a large, plain or coloured surface on the ground and throw paint at it. You can scratch it, rip it, stamp on it, throw mud at it and feel fantastic. You can weep on it, bleed on it, get your dog to dribble on it, roll around on it. Fold it in half, spit on it, drag paint over it and scrape it off again.

You can use just one colour. Or a myriad of colours. You don't have to make a picture. A handcrafted plasticine aeroplane would work just as well. Or yellow. You could paint yellow all day if you liked. Yellow all day might be just what you need.

Artwork comes from a place of vulnerability. And it is from this place that we can gather our inner strength and resources. Playing with colour or making art is a wonderful leveller. It requires honesty and courage, both of which are easy to lose sight of in grief.

And when we are grieving, even the smallest shift or the seemingly tiniest breakthrough can be a quantum leap. It can be the difference between picturing a never-ending black tunnel in front of you, or picturing a black tunnel in front of you with a faint speck of light at the end of it.

When we are grieving, the tunnel with a faint speck wins hands down. Every time.

Trick #42 dealing with pain

Accepting the pain of living, knowing one's heart will – and should – be broken, is the beginning of wisdom.

David J. Wolpe

Pain must be dealt with. The only way to deal with pain is to feel it. It can be challenging to do this.

Your methods of dealing with pain often go way back to what you learned as you grew up. When you were young and fell off your bike, a bandaid, some of that red stuff on your knee (so that everyone could see the graze) and a hug would make it better. It was finished and dealt with until you had to rip the bandaid off.

As you got older and more cool, bandaids and mercurochrome didn't quite cut it anymore. You had to get up, brush yourself off and pretend that you were okay. Even if you weren't. (Kerry reckons the exception to this rule was that if you broke a bone, you could cry! But she doesn't know why.)

You learned to keep more and more to yourself. In part, this was learning to stand on your own two feet. And now as a teenager, you keep certain things to yourself. You just don't always express your true feelings. Probably, no one emerges from childhood unscarred by some hurt they didn't acknowledge at the time.

These inner scars and unspoken secrets live with you. They make up your secret self along with other precious things – your self-worth and self-esteem and your feelings of being lovable and deserving. Sometimes it seems easier to hide your true feelings – out of sight, out of mind – than to deal with them.

And so you learn to hide your pain. Which is pretty sad because pain doesn't just go away. Old pain, new pain – it all has to be dealt with sooner or later.

Some people are good at getting rid of pain. They do this through playing, talking, fighting, stomping, writing, crying, laughing, learning.

But it's unusual to get rid of it completely. The pain that stays with you can build up over time, becoming twisted and distorted. The pain of grief can seem unbearable. But when your grief also contains leftover pain – stuff you haven't dealt with yet – it becomes bigger still, if that is possible.

So how do you deal with the pain of grief? And how do you deal with old pain? How can you possibly do all this without exploding?

It is possible. And I've got just one word for you: Compost.

Grief is like manure; if you spread it out it fertilises. If you leave it in a big pile, it smells like hell.

Thomas Golden

Compost is smelly and ugly and contains old food scraps and manure. Blowflies and rats love it. Worms work inside it – eating the yucky bits, digesting them and turning them out to make wonderful fertiliser. This fertiliser assists in growing vegies, flowers, trees – all the things in the earth's garden which sustain new life and enrich our world. Compost feeds new life. The biggest, most magnificent rainforests began as tiny seeds.

How does this relate to dealing with pain? It's very simple. You compost the pain of your grief. Old grief, new grief. All of it. You do this by releasing your pain gently onto the compost heap.

Composting means looking at your pain instead of burying it. Allowing it to come to the surface and acknowledging it's there. You confront your feelings. You feel them. To the very core and depth of your being, you feel your pain. By doing this, you stop your pain from festering and maggots from breeding in it.

To make good, healthy compost you need to turn it, nurture it and feed it with scraps. Tend to your pain by acknowledging your feelings. Feed it with tears, or solitude, or sadness, screaming, or swearing, or punching bags.

Use the tricks in this book.

When you recycle your pain, you allow for a new beginning inside. You stop being stuck.

When you compost, it's possible to look at how your pain has affected your behaviour. Perhaps it has caused you not to cry in front of others. Or to keep your true feelings a secret. Maybe you didn't want to look weak or uncool in front of your mates, or you wouldn't let your emotions show.

What is the worst thing you can imagine about pain? That it will hurt? That it will never go away? That it will stop you from doing something, or being something? That people will laugh if they see you in an emotional state? That you will feel like a fool? That you will cause someone to dislike you, or lose respect for you? That you will be cast out of your peer group? That you will experience isolation? That you won't be able to deal with the emotions that arise? That you will never recover? That it will haunt you for the rest of your life?

When you compost your pain, you rebalance yourself. Fears, such as those above, are made smaller. Composting also gives you new angles and views on what has happened so that you can gain a new perspective.

From my perspective, here are a few home truths about pain.

Facts about pain.

Physical pain is one of the few things that we cannot 'bring back' or recall. We can associate emotions with it, but we cannot relive physical pain.

Pain never lasts forever. Pain begins and ends. We might have memory of pain, but its intensity diminishes with time.

The anticipation of pain is almost always worse than the actual pain. Think about planning a trip to the dentist for a tooth extraction. Anticipation of pain is the killer.

There are very few pains that we cannot survive. Living in the intensity of them can be uncomfortable, but in general we survive them.

Pain encourages us to live to our potential. It reminds us that we are human, and that time is precious. It illuminates things for us.

In every situation involving pain, there is a pearl of wisdom or a discovery to be found.

With this discovery, the pain may well diminish.

Trick #43 cry baby

I once ran away by myself for a whole weekend just to cry – much to the distress of protective friends and family. I filled quite a few buckets.

Crying is an intensely healing thing to do. It releases endorphins which make you feel better. They're similar to the ones released in laughter, which is why sometimes when you begin an emotional reaction by laughing, you end up crying. And vice versa.

Trick #44 touch

Touch is an incredibly powerful means of communication. It is simply an exchange of energy – no words are required. We never stop needing that human contact. In times of grief, it is common to feel so completely alone that it hurts. Physically, it hurts. The power of touch can assist with healing this pain.

However, in our crazy mixed-up lives, physical contact means different things to everyone. What is a simple hug to one person might be an invitation for kissing to someone else. To interpret people's signals regarding physical contact can be confusing to say the least.

At appropriate times, the power of touch to provide solace and healing is immeasurable. A gentle touch on the hand might comfort someone in a dark place.

When I was lying in traction and had movement in only one arm, all I wanted to do was to touch people's face and hands. This could have been terribly disconcerting for my visitors – luckily, I was able to control my urges!

I also desperately wanted to feel the sensation of running water over my head and hands, and freshly mowed grass underfoot. My heart's strongest desires in my time of crisis were things to do with touch.

As with all of the tricks in this book there are good times and bad times to employ touch. The contact that we might think of offering – a literal shoulder for leaning on, a reassuring pat on the back, a gentle touch to the arm or a full-on hug – each has its time and place.

When you need space around you, there is nothing worse than to be fending off huge bear hugs from well-intentioned visitors. But it can be devastating when you want to hold someone and you are pushed away. In order to avoid either of these awkward meetings, let's look at some issues surrounding personal space.

Firstly, you cannot take away a person's pain by touching them. Your natural human instinct, on seeing another person expressing their pain – particularly when they are crying – is to want to make it better. You want to wrap them up in a bandage or do whatever it takes to fix them. It's really hard to watch someone who's in pain. And people in pain need the space to express it. When a person is sobbing, they don't need to be told to stop. Yet how often do we hear just that? 'Stop crying. Everything will be okay.' Bollocks to that! We need to cry. We have to cry. It's a release, a necessity.

There are certain situations where its best not to interfere – that is, to let a feeling or emotion run its natural course. Remember, it's necessary to feel the pain in order to move through it.

If someone is having a quiet little weep and they know you're around and are comfortable with you, then probably to touch them gently on the shoulder or the arm would be okay. You possibly wouldn't need to say anything – your touch would let them know that you are there and open to listen if they need to talk. And you do need to be prepared to listen if this opens up a conversation.

If a friend or relative has been 'missing' for some time, and you hear muffled cries from behind a closed bedroom door, the signs are that this person needs some space. They probably won't be receptive to physical comfort, no matter how well intentioned, and should not be given a bear hug. If you are worried for their safety, then knock gently before you open the door a crack. You might ask something along the lines of, 'Is there anything I can get you?' and then leave them to it if they are physically okay. A person in this situation needs to be alone.

If you thought there was more to the situation – that they might hurt themselves, for example – you would need to seek professional help.

To hug or be hugged can provide more solace than many hours of discussion, self-analysis and misery. All human beings need the warmth and comfort of others. Touch – in the appropriate time and space and in a form that is comfortable for the giver and receiver – is particularly lovely.

Trick #45 dirt therapy

Dig a garden.

Plant a garden. In the earth, or in pots.

Get your hands dirty. Squelch the dirt through your fingers. Make mud.

Grow vegies. Grow a tree. Grow some flowers.

Nurture your garden.

Hum a little tune to your seeds and plants as you go.

Trick #46 letting others in

Allowing people to care for you can be confronting. Some of us love to be looked after and pampered – and some of us just want to be left alone. Often in a situation of grief, we need to let others in by being open and honest.

Jarrah's homework

Jarrah was 12 and in Year Seven at school. He didn't want his life to change too much by going to high school – he was doing all he could to fit in with his mates and not stand out from the crowd.

He had two friends who had been to primary school with him, and there were another six mates who he had begun hanging out with at high school. It was good. They mucked around at recess and lunchtime, sometimes kicked a footy around the oval and hung it on the girls.

School seemed pretty good.

Before Christmas, Jarrah had told his mates that his dad was gonna leave home. Time had passed with the summer holidays, and then they'd all fronted up to high school. No one had said much about it, really. His new group of mates didn't know about his dad. It was none of their business anyway. Life was just cruising along.

But Jarrah's day-to-day stuff was becoming a bit tricky. Mostly it was okay. He spent weekends with his dad and sometimes one night during the week. The rest of the time he stayed with his mum. Jarrah had no brothers or sisters, so he was lucky that he had his own room and clothes and stuff at each house.

But, one of the problems of living in two houses was that Jarrah kept leaving his homework at his dad's place after the weekend.

He didn't want to ask his dad to bring it over – his parents weren't speaking and Jarrah didn't want to make them more pissed off. So, he just left it.

Also, Jarrah wasn't too sure of how stuff worked with separated parents. He didn't know if it was okay to ask them to do extra things for him. He felt bad about everything.

In the second week of school, Jarrah had a big assignment due which he'd spent a lot of time finishing. But he'd left it at his dad's. Jarrah's teacher stood him up in front of the class – along with another kid – and demanded to know why he hadn't done the assignment. Jarrah said that he'd left it at home. He didn't know what else to say. He felt pretty small.

The teacher didn't seem to believe him.

What a tricky situation!

If Jarrah had been open and honest about his home situation, he might not be in his current predicament. In a way, Jarrah has done the dirty on himself by not being open with his teacher and friends about his present situation. Had they known, they would probably have been more understanding.

Jarrah is in a situation of grief – he has lost the familiarity of his family and home situation, and he's also made the transition from primary to secondary school.

Here's a quick list of some reasons why Jarrah might not have told anyone about his situation:

- It's no one's business
- He doesn't know how to answer their questions
- He wants life to stay normal
- He might lose mates
- He might get into trouble
- Others will think less of him
- Others will make judgments about him and his family
- He doesn't want to talk about it
- School is an escape
- His parents don't want anyone to know
- He can't find the right time to bring it up
- He might cry in front of them if he talks about it
- He doesn't want to lose control
- He doesn't want anyone to have knowledge or power over him
- He wants to ignore it
- He doesn't want sympathy
- It might make the situation worse
- He doesn't know if his mates will handle it well
- He thinks no one really cares about it
- He doesn't want to be the butt of jokes

Letting others in involves sharing. The good stuff, and sometimes, the not so good stuff. The sharing of information can make friendships and other relation-ships stronger. You can feel close to others when you have the courage and guts to talk about how you feel. In friendship, it may also give your mates a chance to understand you a bit better and let them know why you might be angry, moody, irritable or just a bit more stupid than normal! Even when it feels difficult or uncomfortable, it can be really good to let other people in on your grief.

Just talking, as you've seen in previous tricks, can cause your grief to lessen a little. You can also choose who to tell and how much to tell. You don't have to 'sell your soul' or tell every little detail – an outline is enough if that's what you're comfortable with.

Being open with people can help you through a tricky time. It can help your friends too.

Trick #47 time heals all wounds – or does it?

Grief is timeless. Time, in and of itself, doesn't heal grief. But time plus the tricks in your bag can begin the healing process.

Grief is like the wind. When it's blowing hard, you adjust your sails and run before it. If it blows too hard, you stay in the harbour, close the hatches and don't take calls. When it's gentle, you go sailing, have a picnic, take a swim.

Barbara Lazear Ascher

Are you tired of waiting in the longest fast food queue? Do you hate it when you try to ring someone and they're engaged? Do you swear at the computer when it takes too long?

If a slow computer dial-up is bugging you, you'll need some patience. But if you're in a grief situation you'll need a lot of patience, because you can't fast-forward grief.

Almost every single facet of the grieving process requires time. Grieving well takes time. Time and energy. Time and growth. Our grief will not just fly into the wind and away. Nor is grief there all the time. Sometimes we experience it in little fragments. At other times, it hits us like a full-force gale. We need to respect the different forms grief takes, and be patient when it requires more of our energy. We need to be patient with our grief. We must give ourselves time and space to heal.

The cycle of grief has its own timetable. Until that cycle is honoured and completed we are moving along life's path with an anchor down.

Ann Linnea

How do you go about acquiring this patience when you're angry? When all you want to do is smash plates? Or heads, for that matter. What happens when you're so frustrated you can't communicate at all?

Give yourself some time. Use the tricks in this book.

Take a step sideways; take some time out. In a state of grief loads of emotions can wash over you all at once, taking over your body and invading your mind before you're aware of what you are doing or saying. It's easy to lash out at people. It's not usually a conscious decision, but lots of us do it. Make the decision to be patient with yourself and those around you.

Trick #48 daydreaming and meditation

The best and most beautiful things in the world cannot be seen or even touched. They must be felt with the heart.

Helen Keller

You do not need to burn incense, sit cross-legged on a coloured rug or have hairy armpits to meditate. Although, of course, no one would stop you if you wanted to. Sometimes people freak out a bit at the thought of meditation. There is absolutely nothing spooky about it. It is just a means of quieting the mind. As with any other learned skill, there are a number of different methods and approaches to meditation. And there are loads of books, CDs, videos, DVDs and classes devoted to these.

It doesn't really matter how you do it, just as long as you achieve the desired effect of promoting peace and well-being. Meditation helps your mind rest, and it can give you renewed mental focus and clarity. Often the body experiences a deep relaxation.

Meditate.
Live purely. Be quiet.

Do your work with mastery.
Like the moon, come out
From behind the clouds!
Shine.

Buddha

The meditation that I do helps to stop the flow of incessant chatter in my mind.

It doesn't work if I'm thinking about what to cook for dinner or trying to remember the punchline of a joke.

Similarly, I have to remove myself from the other demands of my life. I can't meditate if a child is waving a toy truck under my nose or wanting me to go for a walk. So one of the first needs for meditation is a space to do it in. Remember that your goal is a quiet mind, so somewhere quiet where you won't be interrupted is preferable. It may be indoors or outdoors.

Somewhere comfortable is good. I often fall asleep if I lie down, so I find that sitting is better. I know of people who sit on the edge of a wooden chair so that they don't drift off to sleep.

Initially, it is probably easier to teach yourself meditation with your eyes closed so that you won't be distracted. Some people like to put on relaxation music.

So what happens now?

You visit yourself.

With your eyes closed let the quietness of your surroundings settle. This will generally take a few moments. Take a few very deep breaths. Settle again.

At this point, you will become aware that many thoughts pass through your mind. Don't try to stop these – you won't be able to. Instead try to observe them without a reaction. This may sound a lot easier to do than it actually is. It might help if you imagine yourself to be sitting up high – on top of a diving board or on a cloud – and watch your thoughts as they float past underneath you.

Detach yourself from your thoughts. Try not to react to them emotionally. Allow your thoughts to pass in and out of your field of vision. How much time is there between your thoughts? Can you make another thought drift into your mind?

Settle into your meditation space and relax your body. Take some deep breaths. Become aware of your physical body, and consciously relax any areas of tension. Look specifically at the forehead and shoulders as possible tension areas. Once you are completely relaxed, turn your attention to your thoughts.

Allow one or two to drift past.

And now, instead of simply watching your thoughts, imagine that you are sitting somewhere that you feel comfortable under a blue sky. Picture big, fluffy white clouds drifting gently by on the breeze. Effortlessly.

Each cloud now represents a thought, floating into and out of your field of vision. The big, fluffy white clouds contain no emotional baggage. You do not need to react to them at all, except to observe them as they float past.

White clouds in a brilliant blue sky. Mmmmmm.

I enjoy changing the blues of the sky when I engage in this visualisation, and find it to be a very gentle and centring exercise.

Nature is also a good setting for meditation. I live beside a river in native bushland. It's very conducive to happy meditations! I often find myself simply staring out of the window at the trees and the sky for substantial lengths of time. Sometimes more than half an hour will pass and I will have no recollection of it. Although technically this may not fit the definition of meditation, I find it relaxing and immensely therapeutic. I do it often.

I also love walking through the bush or along a quiet path, keeping my mind and my conscious awareness solely on my footsteps – one in front of the other.

What happens is simply shifting to a different space with the wind and the sky. The skies seem to be very big where I live – they stretch out forever. If I'm not trying too hard, or worrying, my mind is at a place where it can happily switch off. I like to think this happens through meditation. Or perhaps I'm just spacey – who knows for sure!

The benefits of meditating every day are quite phenomenal. Begin with short meditations, say 10 or 15 minutes, and as you become more comfortable with it, build up to 30 minutes or longer.

People who believe meditation is a means of helping to rid the body of disease have been known to meditate for hours at a time. In certain Eastern religions, meditation is the equivalent of, say, going to work. Full days are spent in meditation.

Sit down and meditate. Don't think about it too much, just do it. It gets easier as you become used to it. Switch off your mind, just for a little while. Give yourself a break and some healing at the same time.

Trick #49 I think I can, I think I can

What lies behind us and what lies before us are tiny matters compared to what lies within us.

Oliver Wendell Holmes

Henry Ford (as in Ford cars) said: 'If you think you can – if you think you can't – you're right.'

In other words, believe in yourself.

From the age of 12 years, and for reasons I don't remember, I decided to believe that I could not draw or paint. When offered a tray of potted paints or a box of inviting looking crayons, I would say no thank you. Over the years this grew into a deep-seated belief. I had convinced myself that I just wasn't a visual artist.

It wasn't until I was 25 and had survived a bout with death, that I even thought about challenging this belief that was buried inside me. It wasn't until all my usual outlets for creative expression had become too hard that I thought about having a go at painting. I didn't want to act from a wheelchair, sing with no voice or play the piano with one hand.

I took up the challenge. It was very tricky moving those beliefs that had always told me I wasn't good enough. But I did move through these obstacles. And now I even sell my paintings.

What changed? And how? I could very easily have gone through my entire life with a painting block.

My life circumstances caused me to look at and revise my belief system. What had been true for me in the past (that I was no good at art) was not serving me well. It was blocking me and needed to be re-assessed.

My belief in myself and faith in my decision to change was enough to enable me to turn the corner. If you have faith in yourself, then anything becomes possible. If you think you can, if you think you can't, you're right.

Faith takes so many forms, religious and otherwise, that it's impossible to pigeonhole it. My definition may be totally different to yours, but at its base, faith is about believing and trusting in someone or something.

There are many things that you can have faith in.

You can have faith that you'll be okay in a situation, even when the road is rocky. You can have faith that you're a good person. You can have faith that you have the strength to get through. You can have faith in your belief that people are good. You can have faith in your own abilities and strengths.

Things do change. Perhaps the black hole of grief inside you will never be completely filled in. But it won't stay an open wound forever. You have the power to take steps to close this wound – to leave a healed scar. If you have faith that you will move through life's challenges, if you have faith that the coping strategies or tricks you have chosen to employ will work, if you have faith that your life will move forward, then so be it. That is what will happen. Believe in yourself.

Activating this belief requires a conscious choice or decision on your part. Try speaking the following affirmations over and over again, every day.

'I choose to trust in my ability to make decisions.'

'I choose to move through this challenge with ease.'

'I choose to employ coping strategies that will work in the best possible way for me.'

'I choose to move forward in my life.'

Your choice, your decision.

Once you choose to move forward, then things just seem to fall into place. It's like magic. The strength behind you is always greater than the challenge in front of you.

Trick #50 the gift of giving

Giving is a gift to both the giver and the receiver. It benefits everyone. It also gives you a chance to make sad feelings go away for a time. Giving makes you feel good, and gives you joy. It stops you focusing on yourself, and allows you to look outwards and remember that you are part of a community.

The nature of grief is that it makes you feel insignificant and insecure.

The giving of gifts can give you a sense of meaning and purpose in your life, even for a short time. It allows you to feel needed or important or special or talented or worthwhile, and you remember what it is to experience joy and happiness, even momentarily. And these are very important things to feel, because no one, not even the best and most committed grievers in the world, can stay sad forever. It's just not possible.

There are loads of gifts that you can give. Some of the most precious of these are not tangible things, but the gift of something that will enrich life in a different way. For example, the gift of:

- Space – to sit, to read, to write, to think, to cry, to walk, to breathe and to reflect.
- Time – for fun, for special things, for nothing.
- Dinner – or breakfast, or lunch. Make a delicious, healthy and appetising meal to share.
- A smile – very healing in an appropriate moment.

- A hug – if you both want to. Some people aren't 'touchy feely' like that.
- Help – around the house, with the washing, the shopping and so on.
- Support – a gentle touch on the arm if someone is sad.
- Laughter – a funny movie or a belly laugh.
- Exercise – a walk, or a run, or a gallop.
- Patience – when a person requires something of you.
- Acceptance – the capacity to listen.
- Friendship – sometimes we just need others.

The gift of giving allows you to grieve through 'doing'. It uplifts two people, or more, at once.

Trick #51 help someone else

Do something that's good and right and helpful for someone else. Just for the sake of helping.

Trick #52 staying sane with humour

You're taking the piss, right? Grief and humour? What a joke!

Did you know that it's much easier to smile than to frown? Try it. Smiling uses fewer facial muscles and is much better for you too. You should smile far more often. The healing power of laughter has been well documented.

Laughter reduces the level of stress hormones in our bodies (adrenaline and cortisone). So laughing relieves built-up stress. Just having a good old laugh for 20 seconds uses up as much aerobic energy as if you had rowed a boat, flat out, for two minutes.

After initially raising your heart rate and blood pressure, your whole cardiovascular and respiratory systems go into a lovely relaxed response. This lowered blood pressure and heart rate can last for up to 45 minutes after you laugh.

Laughter is a strong tool for pain relief.

When you laugh, natural endorphins are released from your brain. These make you feel good and improve your immune system.

Amazingly, your brain doesn't know when you're faking it. So even if you're just pretending to laugh at someone's bad joke, you'll still get all the health benefits of laughing.

Your emotion, brain and immune system interactions also apply to negative emotions. So when you watch a horror movie (or even the nightly news) your immune system reacts negatively for from a few days up to a few weeks.

Some hospitals have laughing rooms where patients can laugh themselves well again (provided there are no burst stitches). Then there are laughing groups who meet daily (often before brekkie for a great start to the day) to indulge in some serious giggling.

Powerful healing energies are released during the physical act of laughter. To have happy thoughts is scientifically tested and proven to aid some aspects of physical healing.

It's quite logical if you take the time to think about it. Laughing is such a wonderful feeling. After a good belly laugh, you feel that you can take on the world. Anything becomes possible. Happiness and merriment are the birthrights of every single person on this earth. You deserve to be happy. It's very simple.

So what has this got to do with grief?

Well, everything really. The fact is that no matter how hard you try, you cannot be miserable and depressed forever. It is too exhausting and requires too much energy. Of course you feel sadness in times of grief.

But by enjoying yourself in the moments where you can, you are assisting your own healing to take place. It doesn't mean that you are not experiencing grief. It is certainly not disrespectful. It is a valid and legitimate part of who you are.

An inspirational American doctor, Patch Adams, has been known in his visits to dying people in hospitals to wear a long flowing white robe with huge wings and a glittery halo. Patch is well over six feet tall so he does cause a bit of a stir. To top off his little ensemble, a sign hangs around his neck that reads 'Coming Attractions'. If that doesn't raise a laugh, then nothing will.

Humour helps to break the ice in a number of otherwise difficult situations. I have spent days on 'cancer camps' listening to a tirade of jokes about people's bodies (my own included), where all the campers would be in absolute hysterics.

Importantly, people were making jokes about their own situations rather than being the butt of jokes. Outsiders on these camps may well have found this sort of black humour offensive and very unkind. But it made me feel far less self-conscious to acknowledge my physical being with black humour (I called myself the crip or the spak) than I would have felt had others tiptoed around my very obvious physical condition.

We also bunked down with Hop Along, the lovely Adam with one leg (who played naughty jokes with raw steaks, tomato sauce and carving knives. Lucky the people he played his tricks on all knew that he had only one leg to start with). RIP to you, Adam. Other favourites on camp were Lefty's One and Two

– two guys in their late teens who had each had a right testicle removed.

Humour, in its various guises, is another trick from the old bag.

It's a wonderful coping strategy in the right place and at the right time. Obviously, people's idea of what constitutes funniness is as different as the number of moles on our backs. You never quite know for sure what will tickle another person's funny bone. But in the long run, it really doesn't matter what others think as long as you are not being unkind to them. If it causes someone else to smile, then it's okay. And if it causes us to smile too, then it's even better.

Babies smile from the moment they are born (although unkind theories suggest that it's because they're farting). They also cry from the moment they are born. They cry to survive. They smile because they are enjoying life.

There is a lot of wisdom in little things.

And babies are such lovely little things.

Trick #53 retail therapy

Buy or acquire something simply because. Make it something with intrinsic, inherent beauty. Something that will make you smile whenever you see it. Or be inspired. Or be uplifted. Or feel warm and fuzzy on the inside. Maybe something that smells nice. A budgie. A fish. A crystal. A new outfit. An original artwork. A book. A CD. Your favourite movie on DVD.

The only rule? You have to love it.

Trick #54 talking to yourself

Our deepest fear is not that we are inadequate.
Our deepest fear is that we are powerful beyond
measure.
It is our light, not our darkness, that most frightens
us.
We ask ourselves, who am I to be brilliant, gorgeous,
talented and fabulous?
Actually, who are you NOT to be?

Nelson Mandela

We talk to ourselves in our heads all the time. From shopping lists to singing that tune we heard first thing this morning, to preparing an awkward speech, our minds rarely stop. Self-talk affects how we feel about experiences, and how we respond. Funnily, for something that is with us all the time, we are often unaware of our self-talk.

Self-talk can be either:

Rational: 'I need to get to the station in five minutes or I'll miss the train.' Or

Irrational: 'I should never have moved here, I live so far away from everything, I'll be late for school, the whole class will laugh at me, I'll fail my exams.'

If you talk to yourself rationally about what is going on, life runs in a fairly consistent way. If you talk to yourself irrationally about how things 'should' be, then you might become upset that they aren't a certain way, and you are more likely to feel bad and act in inappropriate ways.

It's helpful to change irrational self-talk to more rational self-talk.

Irrational self-talk contains two parts:
1. The unrealistic expectation: 'I should' or 'He must not'
2. The implied or terrible result: 'Because if I do/don't, then...'

Put together, the sentence could become 'I should not cry (part 1) because if I do, then I must be weak and silly (part 2)'.

If you use rational thought, then you might instead say 'I feel like shit and I'll feel better if I cry.' Instead of feeling angry or stupid or upset, you are now in a better position to accept your feelings and deal with the situation productively.

Used in the right way, self-talk can help you cope with stressful situations. Entire self-help industries revolve around the way that self-talk shapes your life. Often, their solutions involve positive affirmations where you train your self-talk to be uplifting and vibrant. There are examples of these at the end of this trick. Give them a go.

For now though, take some time-out to really listen to your own self-talk. Try making it rational and positive. For me, this was one of the biggest changes I made in my life 'after cancer.' It is quite astounding to tune in to what you're thinking when all of your self-talk is negative. I honestly couldn't believe some of the things I was telling myself, day in and day out.

When in a place of grief, it's common to berate yourself with all sorts of negative thoughts like 'Why didn't I do this differently?', 'If only I hadn't been such a cow', 'I should have known that he was fragile...'

When these sorts of negative thoughts or visions come, acknowledge their existence and then gently but firmly replace them with positive thoughts and images.

An interesting exercise is to monitor your self-talk/thoughts for a minute, or 10 minutes, or over a day and observe whether it's generally positive or negative, helpful or unhelpful. Mine used to be almost completely negative. Subconsciously, I guess that I thought it was okay to squash myself into the mud because it proved that I wasn't 'up myself ' or anything. How tragic is that? All it did was to keep me flat emotionally and stop me living to my full potential.

You alone have the power to change your self-talk. When you make a conscious decision to be positive and self-talk rationally, life takes on a whole new perspective. To this day, if I am feeling a bit down, I look at my self-talk. I repeat little mantras like 'Every day, in every way, life's getting better and better,' and 'I am perfect, whole and complete.' This makes me feel like I'm doing something positive for myself and, by proxy, for those who have to live with me.

Is your self-talk helpful? Look at the table of self-talk and use it as a guide to replace your negative thoughts with more helpful ones. Look into the mirror if you can, and say them while looking yourself square in the eye.

Table of self-talk

Replace this	With this
I deserve to be sad.	Like every other person, I deserve happiness. I am happy.
There is no way out.	The strength inside me will find a way to move through this challenge. I am strong.
I am crap.	I am worthy of love and choose to allow it into my life.
Nobody else knows what I am going through.	I am unique.
I am alone.	I experience life and grief in my own way.
	There is always someone to turn to.

Table 4.2: Your self-talk matters. Make it positive. Make it helpful.

Trick #55 imagination

Sometimes I have believed as many as six impossible things before breakfast.

Lewis Carroll

Escape into the world of imagination. Revisit childhood books like *The Magic Faraway Tree, Mary Poppins, The Hobbit* – books where you can revisit your childhood sense of wonder. Escape through fun movies or fantasy adventures. Set your imagination free!

As you imagine, so it is.

Open up to the idea that anything is possible. As you imagine, so it is. It's possible. What you imagine can become reality. Imagine that you have power over every aspect of your own life. Imagine that your very thoughts and visions might direct your own reality.

If this were so, it would be wise to be selective over what you choose to give your energy to.

As you imagine, so it is.

If this statement is true, the implications are enormous. Each one of us contains incredible potential. Not the least of which is the strength to move through personal life challenges, including grief, with the certainty of a light at the end of that tunnel. Because we can imagine that light!

And the absolutely wonderful thing is, you don't even have to believe that it's true to have a go. Even if you think it's far-fetched, you can try it with nothing to lose. All it takes is an imagination. It's free. Everyone's got one.

Even Albert Einstein, scientist and philosopher, believed in the incredible power of the imagination. He said, 'Imagination is more important than knowledge.'

Imagination is infinite. It has no beginning and no end. It is whatever you instruct it to be.

Use your imagination to transport you out of your grief. Imagine where you will be in a year. In five years. In 10 years.

'I imagine that one day my grief will be easier to deal with.'

'I imagine that one day I'll be sitting on the beach and I'll have a new best friend.'

'I imagine that one day I will tell my own children about their grandpa.'

'I imagine that my life can be wonderful again.'

And so on.

Imagine that there is a light and love that will live on past your grief and its challenges.

Imagine a positive sea of energy gently enfolding you in its warmth.

Imagine your own healing, and the healing of others who are experiencing grief. There is no limit to your imagination.

Moving on – life after grief

One day, I'm gonna grow wings.

Radiohead

Is there life after grief? Will I ever laugh again? Will I ever feel okay again? The very simple answer to these questions is yes. Of course.

According to Kerry Abramowski and Dr Michael Carr-Gregg, grief is healed when you are able to:

- stand in it and not run,
- name it and start to know its comings and goings,
- slow down your pace and find a place to experience your pain within,
- be in your body,
- accept it as a temporary visitor and not think that you are your grief.

You have the tools to assist you with grief now and in the future. You have learned about and built on your own wisdom and strength. You are now in the place where you will create and discover your own future. It is both exciting and daunting. You have your whole life ahead of you. It might be a short life, or it might be a long one. You just don't know. What you do know, is that life needs to be lived every day. For every moment. You know that life is precious and unique, and that human beings have a profound and amazing capacity to touch each other deeply. You know that there are times when you feel like there's a huge black hole inside you.

You know what it is to mourn. You know what it is to feel sorrow at the deepest levels of your being. You know the despair of being so sad that your whole body and being aches. You know the feeling that this may never end.

On top of this, you know that life must be lived, for we all die. You know that you have felt love in life. You know that you have the strength (and the tricks or coping strategies) to deal with, and move through, any situations that arise.

You know that there is a light at the end of the tunnel, even if it's hard for you to see right now.

You know that your grief contributes to who you are today, and that this is a gift. You know that in some way, you will carry with you the situation you are grieving for – be it a person who has died, or a failed relationship, or an unborn child. That you are stronger because of your grief.

You know that you will not forget. You know that your pain will ease, although it may never disappear completely.

You know so many things, but sometimes, this still doesn't help. Sometimes, you just need to remember. To sit by yourself and have a good cry. Or to sing into your hairbrush microphone and be a rock star in the bedroom for a while.

Sometimes, you just need to be.

Your memories are precious. Life is precious.

You keep an aspect of every person who has touched your life inside you. It is with you always. Whether in the form of a cherished memory, a funny saying, a song that repeats itself over and over, or a sense of oneness with them, it makes no difference.

When someone makes it into another's heart, a vibration is established. A resonance. So that when two people communicate on a physical or emotional level, their souls connect as well. This soul connection remains, even when a physical body dies or a friendship ends.

There is a future after grief. You will find your own way. You will do it in your own time. Use the tricks in your bag, and remain open and honest.

You have yourself. And that is a wonderful thing. You are precious and unique, deserving of much happiness.

Armed with your bag of tricks you have the potential to be anything. Your future is waiting for you to create it.

Life is to be lived. It is time to move forward, mindful of your being and of what makes your heart sing.

You will always remember, on some level.

You will live again.

You will cry again.

You will laugh again.

In its own time, your future is your own to create.

Come to the edge, he said.

They said, we are afraid.
Come to the edge, he said.
They came.
He pushed them...
And they flew.

Guillaume Apollinaire

Sharing the grief book

If you're a friend, wrap it in a big fat bow and give it as a gift.

If you're a parent, just leave it lying around near the remote control or in the loo.

If you are a person who cares about someone, be creative – think outside the square and find a way to share it.

If you've claimed it for yourself, we wish you well.

Acknowledgments

This book has been a collaboration in the truest sense of the word. It contains the wisdom and knowledge of many people. Some have been quoted directly, others appear in the form of anecdotes and short stories. Many of these offerings have been inspired by the young people with whom Kerry and I have spent time.

We have incorporated the ideas of numerous re-markable people who also happen to be authors, including Dr Michael 'Prof' Carr-Gregg's original thoughts on issues related to grief and loss in adolescence. Trick #5 – visualise your grief, and trick #26 – the cup, have come directly from his well of information. Thank you Prof, for your insights and wisdom.

From the inimitable Dr Ian Gawler – who has been an inspiration to countless people when they have needed hope – we have taken meditation ideas and clues for success.

Kenneth Doka's work on rituals has been incorpo-rated into our section on healing and releasing. Heartfelt gratitude goes out to these people.

Much of our own 'wisdom' has come directly from sharing with young people. People we admire, respect, miss dreadfully. People with whom we have lived hilarious, sad, touching and sometimes even ludicrous moments.

To all who have contributed – as part of a short story or anecdote, and some in ways mere words will never do justice to – thank you.

And finally, a big fat thank you to the people who have been so supportive throughout the writing and rewriting of this book. It's been quite an adventure.

Elizabeth Vercoe and Kerry Abramowski

Sources

Books, journals and poems
Joan Chittister, *Gospel Days: Reflections for Every Day of the Year*
Mark Twain, 'Old Times on the Mississippi', *Atlantic Monthly, 1875*
Helen M. Luke, *The Way of Woman*
Terry Kettering, *The Elephant in the Room*
Richard Bach, *Illusions*
Richard Bach, *Illusions*
Mary Margaret Funk, *Thoughts Matter*
Erica Jong, *How to Save Your Own Life*
David Wolpe, *Making Loss Matter*
Barbara Lazear Ascher, *Landscape Without Gravity: A Memoir of Grief*
Ann Linnea, *Deep Water Passage: A Spiritual Journey at Midlife*
Oliver Wendell Holmes in Jon Kabal-Zinn, *Wherever You Go, There You Are*

Songs

Badly Drawn Boy, 'The Shining', from *The Hour of Bewilderbeast*

Radiohead, 'Let Down', from *OK Computer*

About the authors

about elizabeth vercoe by kerry abramowski

Liz is a teacher, an actor, an artist, receiver of a Queen's Trust award, a volunteer, a mother, a writer and has been described by the press as a 'remarkable cancer survivor'.

Once she gets something in her head, like writing this book, watch out! She has realised the importance of a book such as this for a long time and finally, thankfully, she has now followed through with her convictions.

Diz' or 'Dizo' as I like to call her has changed – a lot. Who wouldn't when you've been through what she has? She was diagnosed with cancer, treated and 'fixed.' It came back – she got VERY sick. She was told she might die. She was told she'd never walk again – may never speak properly again. And that she'd never be able to have children...

Now, she's walking, talking and has three beautiful children.

Dizo is witty, very spiritual, wise, clever and an inspiration for a great many people – she is loved by a great many people. Oh, and one more thing she's calm!

about kerry abramowski by elizabeth vercoe

Kerry is a social worker, although not a very typical one. Over the years she has run CanTeen Victoria (for teenage cancer patients, siblings and children) and Big Brothers, Big Sisters (for kids needing a bigger person to spend time with), worked for the Salvos, and now has her own private practice called Grief Relief. Kerry has spent most of her working life assisting people – young people who are sick, who are homeless, who are sad, who are on drugs, who don't have families to talk to. She spends a lot of time training other adults in her areas of expertise.

Kerry likes and respects young people. Kerry listens to people. All people. And people talk to her. I have seen them lining up to take their turn. She works with skill, intuition and compassion.

The young people she works with both admire and adore her (and sometimes they get mad at her too).

She has a wicked sense of humour and will not hesitate to laugh raucously when someone trips over. But she will also be the first one to offer them a hand up. This book wouldn't have been written without Kerry and her infamous 'bag of tricks'.

A note about adolescence and grief

As we go through our lives, experiences of loss and grief are not merely possibilities but certainties for us all. Yet, today's society unrealistically portrays childhood and adolescence as a time of unremittent joy and freedom. Loss and grief, when it does come, is often seen as stealthy and unexpected.

Unfortunately, the reality of life all too often brings young people face to face with at least 40 different life experiences which can produce the range of emotions called grief. These include tragic circumstances such as divorce, parental separation, death of their pet, the terminal illness of their parent, their own struggle with life-threatening disease, the accidental death of their sibling, or the suicide of a friend.

The gravity of any of these situations takes young people beyond the innocence of childhood and plunges them into a kaleidoscope of fear and uncertainty. Unfortunately, our perceptions and attitudes toward loss and grief do not equip young people with the tools to help them cope adequately with such overwhelming experiences. In light of this, it is unsurprising that the circumstances surrounding a loss are difficult to handle at any age. Adolescence, however, brings with it challenges and struggles that have been largely overlooked up until recently.

In this unique and compassionate guide, Liz Vercoe and Kerry Abramowski turn their attention to the special needs of adolescents struggling with loss and give them the tools they need to work through their pain and grief.

Given that adolescence has never been more difficult, this book is timely and fills a much needed gap – many of my clients are confused about the emotions they experience following a loss. It seems as though society has hoodwinked many into believing 'time heals all wounds', which it untrue. Time just passes – it takes actions to heal your heart.

I congratulate the authors and black dog books for this contribution. The clear and accessible format that is the hallmark of Liz and Kerry's writing guides teens through the often treacherous emotional terrain that can accompany loss at this vulnerable age. *The Grief Book* offers many 'actions' or tricks that experience has shown work.

The message I hope all young readers take from this extraordinary book is that the human body is a 'processing plant' for emotions, not a container to carry them around. Above all, Liz and Kerry let young people know that even in their darkest hour, they are not alone.

Dr Michael Carr-Gregg PhD MAPS
Adolescent Psychologist
Founder, CanTeen

174

Notes
[space left intentionally blank in the original book]

Also by elizabeth vercoe

Image A

Here is Jess's life so far:
She is 16 years old.
She's never wagged school.
She's on a netball team.
Her best friends are Sara and Charlotte.

She has cancer.
Last week she kissed a boy called Dylan.
Today her hair is going down the plughole.
If Dylan finds out he'll probably
drop her – or worse, feel sorry for her.
Can she keep it a secret?

Praise for *Keep Your Hair On!*
'What, you may ask, is the point of going through a dreadful time if you cannot write a novel about it afterwards? When the writing turns into an excellent novel, it is a bonus.'
The Age
'Compelling reading.'
The Herald Sun
'In a better world, kids wouldn't get cancer and have to deal with chemo, throwing up and having their hair fall out. Unfortunately life is otherwise, and you can only be glad that there are writers like Vercoe, who has herself lived through the experience and is able to write about it. An uplifting book.'
Publishing News, London

By Carole Wilkinson

Image B

Ancient China, Han Dynasty. A slave girl saves the life of an ageing dragon and escapes her brutal master. Pursued by a ruthless dragon hunter, the girl and the dragon cross China carrying with them a mysterious stone that must be protected. This is the story of a young slave girl who believes she is not worthy of a name but finds within herself the strength and courage to make this perilous journey – and do what must be done.

Dragonkeeper
Shortlisted 2004 NSW Premier's Literary Awards
Joint winner 2004 Aurealis Award for speculative
 fiction
Shortlisted 2004 CBCA Book of the Year awards

'A truly fabulous journey. I loved every dragon's tooth, claw and scale of it.'
Gary Crew

By Jutta Goetze

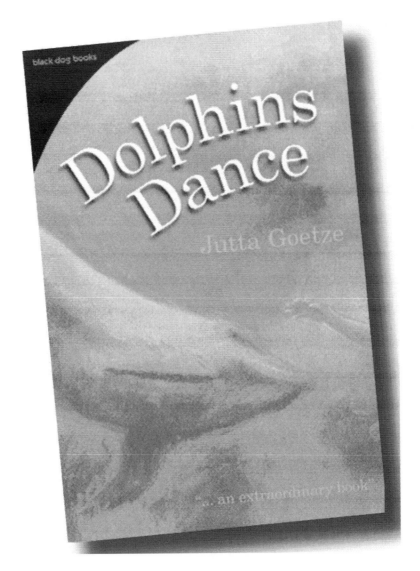

Image C

"You can't see it."

Dad cleared his throat. He was standing in front of Ali's class, about to give a talk.

"It isn't like measles or mumps. It's not like when you break your leg. And it's definitely not catching, like when you get a cold."

Ali listened, her fingers crossed. If her father couldn't make them understand, nobody could.

Ali's younger brother Max has autism. Max will be coming to Ali's school this year and she is not happy. All Ali wants is to fit in – and that's not easy with a brother like Max.

Praise for *Dolphins Dance*
'A sensitive and hopeful book, shedding a lot of light on a difficult and somewhat mysterious subject.'

Magpies

'This is a beautifully written story ... a delightful and valuable read.'
The Sunday Tasmanian
'Thoughtful and direct.'
The Age

Image D

...thank you for reading books from black dog

Back Cover Material

black dog books
Visit us:
www.bdb.com.au

"Grief is like a manure; if you spread it out it fertilises. if you leave it in big pile, it smells like hell."

Here is a book full of practical ideas to help you or somebody you know move through grief.

'A unique and compassionate guide, which gives people struggling with grief and loss the tools they need to work through their grief. Above all, Elizabeth Vercoe and Kerry Abramowski let young people know that even in their darkest hours they are not alone.'

Dr Michael Carr-Gregg

Books For ALL Kinds of Readers

At ReadHowYouWant we understand that one size does not fit all types of readers. Our innovative, patent pending technology allows us to design new formats to make reading easier and more enjoyable for you. This helps improve your speed of reading and your comprehension. Our EasyRead printed books have been optimized to improve word recognition, ease eye tracking by adjusting word and line spacing as well as minimizing hyphenation. Our EasyRead SuperLarge editions have been developed to make reading easier and more accessible for vision-impaired readers. We offer Braille and DAISY formats of our books and all popular E-Book formats.

We are continually introducing new formats based upon research and reader preferences. Visit our web-site to see all of our formats and learn how you can Personalize our books for yourself or as gifts. Sign up to Become A RHYW Registered Reader.

www.readhowyouwant.com